The best fash... ...reet.
Always has been and always will be

and she can conquer the world

MARILYN MONROE

The best thing
about London,
is Paris DIANA
VREELAND

Style is a simple way of saying
complicated things

JEAN COCTEAU

Whoever said that money can't buy happiness,
simply didn't know where to go shopping BO DEREK

One is never over-dressed or underdressed
with a Little Black Dress KARL LAGERFELD

that we have to alter it every six months

OSCAR WILDE

AMBER JANE BUTCHART'S
FASHION
MISCELLANY

AMBER JANE BUTCHART'S

FASHION

⚬— MISCELLANY —⚬

AN ELEGANT COLLECTION OF STORIES, QUOTATIONS, TIPS & TRIVIA FROM ~ THE WORLD OF STYLE ~

ILLUSTRATIONS BY PENELOPE BEECH

THE FASHION MISCELLANY

First published in the UK, US, and Canada in 2013 by
ILEX
210 High Street, Lewes
East Sussex, BN7 2NS
www.ilex-press.com

Publisher: Alastair Campbell
Creative Director: James Hollywell
Managing Editors: Nick Jones and Natalia Price-Cabrera
Senior Editor: Ellie Wilson
Editorial Assistant: Rachel Silverlight
Commissioning Editor: Zara Larcombe
Art Director: Julie Weir
Designer: Lisa McCormick
Picture Research: Katie Greenwood

British Library Cataloguing-in-Publication Data
A catalog record for this book is available from
the British Library.

ISBN: 978-1-78157-138-5

Printed and bound in China

Colour Origination by Ivy Press Reprographics

2 4 6 8 10 9 7 5 3 1

"Give a girl the right shoes and
she can conquer the world."
MARILYN MONROE

TAILORING LINGO

THE MERCHANT TAYLORS' COMPANY was formed by the 14th century. As such it's no surprise that language anomalies have built up around this historic craft. Let us unpick the seams of meaning for you:

FIGURATIONS: The details of your measurements. If you have a dropped shoulder/a stoop/one arm longer than the other—a bespoke suit will disguise these points.

ROCK OF EYE: An innate ability to get shapes and lines and proportion "by eye," without measuring.

KIPPERS: Women employed for buttonholing and finishing (traditionally these women would arrive looking for work in pairs). The contemporary term is Finisher.

COCK KIPPER: A male Finisher.

CABBAGE: Small, useless offcuts; the apprentice could sell to these to the rag-and-bone man to supplement their income.

MUNGO: Rough cloth used to mock up garments that may have many changes to come—similar to a toile in dressmaking.

FIN BAR FIN: The construction of a jacket is complete but none of the finishing has been done.

FIN BAR CUFF: A jacket is finished except for the cuff holes so minor adjustments can still be made.

LAY: How you lay pattern on cloth to maximize its usage.

BAISTING: Temporary stitching used to hold a garment together for the first fitting.

"Women think of all colors except the absence of color. I have said that black has it all. White too. Their beauty is absolute. It is the perfect harmony." COCO CHANEL

A DOT BY ANY OTHER NAME

ALTHOUGH SIMPLE BY design, the use of dots as a clothing pattern or adornment has a relatively short history, due to early associations of spots, or flecking, with disease.

In the 16th and 17th centuries they were adopted through the practice of "moucheron" (French for "little fly") or patching: beauty spots made of black taffeta or velvet to cover blemishes or draw attention to preferred features.

Reminiscent of spotty Flamenco dress with its Andalusian, Gypsy, and Moorish roots, it was another dance—the Polka—that truly popularized the design. Although the association between the dance and dots is unclear, the Polka fad swept Europe then America in the mid-19th century. Originating in Slavic areas of Central Europe, the Polka spread to Paris, and then like wildfire crossed the Channel and the Atlantic by the 1840s.

Quick to cash in on a craze, canny marketeers began selling a range of products with a "Polka" theme, but it was the dots to which the name stuck, and *Godey's* magazine featured one of the earliest mentions of it in 1871. The pattern became a favorite during the 1950s, aided by Christian Dior's designs and immortalized in Brian Hyland's 1960 hit "Itsy Bitsy Teenie Weenie Yellow Polka Dot Bikini."

BABY BLUES

THINKING OF DRESSING your little girl in pink or your little boy in blue? The "pink for girls, blue for boys" rule has actually been around for less than 100 years. Before then girls were expected to wear blue, as the paler color, and boys were encouraged to wear pink, traditionally seen as the "stronger" color, as it's closer to red.

A BRIEF HISTORY OF THE HIGH HEEL

STURDY FOOTWEAR IS THOUGHT to have developed between 40,000 and 26,000 years ago, and shoes—especially heels—hold an important place in folktales across the world and throughout history. The Cinderella story exists in many forms, with the footwear varying according to local traditions, from golden shoes in 9th century China to fur boots, jeweled shoes, and even galoshes in Denmark. Shoes have long had symbolic, as well as practical value; with that in mind, here is a brief guide to high heels.

Throughout history shoes have often been associated with social standing, as demonstrated by the saying "well heeled" in reference to the wealthy. Early Greek actors wore platform sandals called kothorni made of wood and cork that were constructed in various heights to denote the social status of different characters—a very visual representation of class.

Next came the qabaqib. These were worn by Turkish women in bathhouses to elevate them above the heated floors, a very practical solution. A similar device originated in medieval Europe with the patten: this was an overshoe to protect the wearer from the filth of the streets in a time before proper sewage systems or street paving. So heel height hasn't always been associated with glamour!

Ottoman dress (see the qabaqib above) inspired many European fashions, and some historians believe that this led to the next development in Europe—the chopine. This was a type of women's platform shoe that was popular in the 15th, 16th, and 17th centuries, especially in Venice where they were known as zoccoli. Initially they were used as a covering to protect the shoes or the dress from, again, the mud and filth of the streets—but they soon reached heights that far outweighed their use as protection.

At these extreme heights, chopines became an aesthetic reminder of status. They were so high that servants were needed on either side of the wearer for support, and as such they were used by noble women of patrician families to symbolize their wealth. They were also worn under long gowns—all the longer for the height of the chopine—which

required extra fabric to cover them and again indicated the financial wherewithal of the wearer. Courtesans took to the style, swiftly leading to sumptuary laws which prohibited them from wearing chopines, and even from wearing silk dresses and virtually all jewelry at certain times.

Chinese shoes are historically associated with the practice of foot-binding, but what's less well-known is the Manchu "flower pot" or "horse hoof" shoes of the imperial court. In 1644 the Ching dynasty came to power, the last in Chinese history. The dynasty was ruled by Manchus, a nomadic group that came from the north, and much of what we know today as Chinese material culture developed during this period, including clothing, such as the long robe called a qipao or cheongsam. The Manchus didn't practice footbinding, preferring instead that their women were given extra height through the "flower pot" shoe. Somewhat precarious as footwear, the wearer would take wide strides, swinging the arms for balance.

After the French Revolution, heeled shoes—which had been worn by both men and women at court—fell out of favor. Associated with the opulent excess of the French aristocracy, flat shoes were all the rage, symbolizing a "leveling out" of society.

The 19th century Adelaide boot was the epitome of Victorian modesty, despite being developed before Victoria took the throne. Named after Adelaide, the Queen Consort of King William IV (1830–37), the  flat boot was popular from its introduction in the 1830s until the front-lacing boot took its place two decades later. Reaching up to the ankle, the boots proved especially useful in the 1850s when the newly developed crinoline replaced full petticoats as the undergarment of choice. Crinolines, though lighter than multiple petticoats, were susceptible to the vagaries of the wind and so were liable to lift up, exposing the pesky ankles in a way deemed most obscene by prudish Victorians. Thankfully the ankle-covering Adelaide boot preserved modesty. As the shoes were more frequently on display, they were often dyed with the bright aniline synthetic colors that were being developed at the same time.

With many design innovations people often argue over who was the original creator, and such is the case with the stiletto heel. The debate rages on, but the style is most often associated with Roger Vivier, who worked for Christian Dior in the 1950s. His needle-like heel debuted in 1954 and quickly became associated with Dior's New Look from 1947—which was a return to an almost Victorian silhouette that emphasized femininity in the postwar drive to get women back into the home. Dior's H Line from 1954 emphasized slimness, far from the Rosie the Riveter images and boxy tailoring of the war years. The stiletto signified sex appeal, status, and luxury in the economic boom of the 1950s. Roger Vivier also made the jewel-encrusted shoes for Queen Elizabeth II's coronation in 1953.

The rise of glam rock in the 1970s led to the resurgence of platform shoes, and they were adopted by both men and women. Historically, high-heeled shoes have been worn by men for various reasons, from horse riding to conferring status and power on the wearer. Iconic shoes designers like Terry de Havilland were in effect bringing equality back to the high heel. Terry was taught to cobble by his father, who ran a shoemaking business and sold platform heels to showgirls at the Windmill club during the war.

Heels are notorious for going up and down in fashion, from the towering—think Naomi Campbell taking a tumble on the runway for Vivienne Westwood in a pair of nine inch mock-croc platforms called the "Super Elevated Ghillie" in 1993—to the kitten heel. But something about the color red has always intrigued shoemakers. Christian Louboutin learnt his craft by watching showgirls dance and wanting to make shoes for them; his designs—immediately identifiable by their blood red sole—are some of the most covetable in the world today. The red sole is trademarked to Louboutin—a canny branding move as it means you can easily spot his shoes from afar. It was the subject of a lawsuit in 2012 when Louboutin sued Yves Saint Laurent—who had created a red shoe—for copyright infringement. Yves Saint Laurent were triumphant, but only

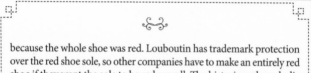
because the whole shoe was red. Louboutin has trademark protection over the red shoe sole, so other companies have to make an entirely red shoe if they want the sole to be red as well. The historic and symbolic qualities of red shoes were even noted by Yves Saint Laurent's lawyers, who referenced the red-heeled shoes of Sun King Louis XIV and the ruby slippers of *The Wizard of Oz* during the court case.

CHARLES WORTH:
THE MAN WHO INVENTED GOOD TASTE

DID YOU KNOW that it was a British man who invented the haute couture system in France?

Charles Frederick Worth was born in Lincolnshire in 1825, and in his youth worked for various London textile mills. In 1845 he moved to Paris and became a salesman for a textile goods company. After much success in this area, he opened a dressmaking department for the company and eventually branched out into his own business in 1858. Luckily for Worth his foray into fashion occurred at the same time that the Second Empire in France was instated. Paris was once again an imperial capital, and the subsequent flurry of state events and balls left many women in need of fine dressing. The demand for luxury textiles grew, and the Emperor's wife, Empress Eugenie, set the styles at court. Eugenie favored Worth's designs and her patronage was instrumental in his success.

What was revolutionary about Worth was that he designed pieces seasonally; before Worth, women with means would employ a dressmaker to create items to their taste. In designing the garments himself, Worth dictated what was "good taste" and, along with his use of live models to display his goods, he essentially put the wheels in motion for the fashion system that remains with us today.

"Fashion is not something that exists in dresses only. Fashion is in the sky, in the street, fashion has to do with ideas, the way we live, what is happening." COCO CHANEL

···· ANTI-FASHION AND RATIONAL DRESS ····

A S WITH YOUTH SUBCULTURES, which are often defined by their resistance to and subversion of mainstream style, many groups throughout history have refused to be slaves to fashion's dictates.

The Rational Dress Society was established by Lady Harberton in 1881. A big fan of cycling, Lady Harberton believed clothing should be non-restrictive and practical. As such she favored boneless stays over tight-laced corsets, and she also held the opinion that women shouldn't have to wear more than seven pounds of undergarments. The idea of dress reform was a popular one in the face of the constrictive styles of the Victorian era.

Amelia Bloomer had advocated women wearing bifurcated, baggy, Turkish-style trousers under knee-length skirts in the 1840s and 1950s, and had been so enthusiastic that the item became known as "Bloomers." But the popular press ran so many anti-Bloomerism pieces that she renounced the style as it was distracting attention from her work in women's rights.

In 1884 the first Jaeger store opened, promoting the idea of wearing animal, rather than plant, fibers next to the skin. Opened by Lewis Tomalin, the store—initially called Dr Jaeger's Sanitary Woollen System—was inspired by the work of Dr Gustav Jaeger, a hygienist and naturalist who believed that wools were more breathable and healthy next to the skin than plant-based fabrics such as cotton.

In the early 20th century manifestos on both men's and women's clothing were written by the Italian Futurism movement. These dictates set out to banish "funereal" black and to create clothing that was functional but also colorful. With its championing of utilitarian styles and bright colors it arguably foreshadowed the rise of sportswear throughout the remainder of the century.

Fast forward to the 1930s and a group of men began campaigning for more beauty and practicality in menswear. Soon the Men's Dress Reform Party was born, which promoted shorts or kilts over the wearing of trousers, as well as lighter, washable fabrics and less stiff formality as embodied by items like collar studs. Again the movement provided a taster of the eventual rise of sportswear that would dominate the end of the 20th century and the beginning of the 21st.

FASHIONABLE FURNITURE

CONCEPTUAL FASHION DESIGNER HUSSEIN CHALAYAN often harnesses the power of technology in his collections. In 2000 he surprised the fashion world by creating a transforming wooden coffee-table skirt, ensuring the models literally walked off the catwalk wearing parts of the set.

> "I loathe narcissism, but I approve of vanity."
> DIANA VREELAND

FASHION THAT NEVER GROWS UP

THE PETER PAN COLLAR has been a style staple that has appealed to mods of the 1960s through to the indie styles of Alexa Chung. It was given its name when it played a starring role in one of the earliest *Peter Pan* stage shows in 1905. Maude Adams was the first actress to play Peter Pan on Broadway. Her costume consisted of feathered cap and leafy breeches with a large pristine white collar falling to her shoulders. The style has been known as the Peter Pan collar ever since.

LET'S GET DIGITAL: KEY MOMENTS IN FASHION ON THE INTERNET

1998: Helmut Lang replaced his catwalk show with a virtual show on his website, the first time a fashion show occurs online.

1999: The first online fashion magazine, *Ntouch*, is launched by London College of Fashion.

JUNE 2000: ASOS.com—now the UK's largest independent fashion retailer—is launched, initially to e-tail clothes inspired by celebrities (As Seen On Screen). A Facebook shop is launched in 2011.

SEPTEMBER 2000: style.com, respected fashion hub and home of catwalk critics, is launched.

2000: Influential fashion photographer Nick Knight establishes SHOWstudio.com, with a continuing commitment to pushing the boundaries of fashion online.

2000: High-end e-tailer Net-A-Porter is launched. Natalie Massenet initially funded the venture through help from friends and family as it was seen as such a risky venture. It was sold to luxury holding company Richemont in 2010 for £350 million.

2003: NoGoodForMe.com—the first fashion blog—begins.

2004: Bryan Grey Yambao (now known as Bryan Boy) begins blogging from his home in Manilla, Philippines. In 2008 Marc Jacobs saw a fan video BryanBoy had posted, and named a green ostrich bag "BB" in his honor. He's been a front row fixture at every Marc Jacobs show (and many others) since.

2005: Scott Schuman starts his streetstyle blog thesartorialist.com.

MARCH 2006: Self-confessed "fashion outsider" Susanna Lau sets up her StyleBubble blog. She subsequently became one of the figureheads of the generation of bloggers that took the fashion world by storm in the late noughties. It would lead to fashion insider jobs at Dazed Digital and writing for established print magazines such as *Elle*.

NOVEMBER 2006: dazeddigital.com, the online arm of Jefferson Hack's publishing empire, is founded.

2006: Yvan Rodic starts posting his streetstyle snaps at his blog, Facehunter. blogspot.com.

FEBRUARY 2007: Micro-blogging platform Tumblr is launched. Within two weeks the service has 75,000 users, including a strong following in the fashion community.

2007: Website The Business of Fashion is set up by former management consultant Imran Amed. In February 2013 it was awarded £1.3 million in funding from investors including Louis Vuitton Moet Hennessy.

2007: Fashion blogging is given industry validation as Chanel invite twelve bloggers to Paris for a weekend of discovering "the history and iconic places of Chanel."

2008: Style Rookie blog is set up by an 11 year old Tavi Gevinson.

SEPTEMBER 2008: Jak and Jil streetstyle blog is launched by Tommy Ton. With a trademark focus on details he quickly forges a unique aesthetic that soon sees commissions from style.com and *GQ* among others.

JANUARY 2010: Paula Reed, style director of *Grazia*, tweets a picture of her view at the Dior couture show which has been obscured by an enormous bow in Tavi Gevinson's hair. The backlash against FROW bloggers begins, and highlights the shifting field of fashion journalism as well as friction between old and new media.

FEBRUARY 2010: British heritage brand Burberry live stream their Autumn/Winter 2010 catwalk show from London Fashion Week on their website, and simultaneously stream it in 3D at spaces in New York, Paris, Dubai, Tokyo, and LA.

MARCH 2010: Pinterest is launched. Within two years it becomes the fastest site in history to break through the ten million unique visitor mark.

OCTOBER 2010: Photo sharing app Instagram is launched.

DECEMBER 2010: *POST Matter* is launched—the first culture magazine created exclusively for the iPad with no print or web-based supplement.

FEBRUARY 2011: Burberry continue to democratize the catwalk show by screening their collection online, on the iPhone and iPad, and also on a screen at Piccadilly Circus and at global flagship stores in real time.

2011: MA Fashion Media Production launched at London College of Fashion to bridge traditional disciplines such as journalism and photography with digital and new media practices.

APRIL 2012: Nick Knight conducts the first fashion photoshoot on Instagram. Using model-of-the-moment Cara Delevingne and inspired by internet meme culture and the craze for animal GIFs, the shoot takes filter-based photography apps into high fashion for the first time.

FEBRUARY 2013: Topshop Unique partnered with Google+ to live stream their Autumn/Winter 2013 from all angles.

POIRET: THE ONE THOUSAND AND SECOND NIGHT PARTY

IN THE EARLY 20TH CENTURY couturier Paul Poiret took the fashion world by storm with his scant regard for corsetry and his fantastical Orientalist styles. He was a true pioneer in many areas, the marketing of fashion being one that he excelled at. He was one of the first designers to really embrace the mannequin parade—the forerunner of the catwalk show—and he was a born showman in his quest for publicity.

In June 1911 he organized a party to capitalize on the "Eastern" trend he initiated, with the apt title of the One Thousand and Second Night party. The gala was held in the gardens next to Poiret's Paris mansion and the invites stipulated that an appropriate costume was non-negotiable. He cannily had rails of his latest collection lined up by the entrance, ready to adorn any party-goer who had ignored the dress code. Poiret himself dressed as Sultan Poiret the Magnificent and greeted guests from beneath a blue canopy embellished with his initials. His wife Denise became a captive beside him in an enormous gilded cage, resplendent in harem pants and a jeweled bustier of Poiret's creation.

Poiret vehemently discredited the claim that his work was derivative of the Eastern-themed productions of the Ballets Russes, but there's no denying that his party and subsequent collections had a touch of Diaghilev and Bakst's Schéhérazade to them.

> "A woman's dress should be like a barbed-wire fence: serving its purpose without obstructing the view."
> SOPHIA LOREN

FROM THE BOER WAR TO BOGART:
THE LIFECYCLE OF THE TRENCH COAT

FROM THE TRENCHES of the Great War to detectives in pulp fiction potboilers, the trench coat has always suggested the darker side of human nature. Not to be confused with earlier macs (from Charles Macintosh—now synonymous with any waterproof jacket), the trench coat has become a staple of the autumn wardrobe, a perennial on the catwalk that's reinvented nearly every season. Though most people associate the coat with the First World War (hence the name), it was actually the Boer war in the late 19th century that introduced officers to what would later become the full-fledged trench. Developed by Thomas Burberry, its weather-proof gabardine fabric, precise cut, and practical details soon ensured it became the officer's jacket of choice. When 1914 came around, Burberry was commissioned by the War Office to adapt the design for the new combat necessities of the trenches. He added a few extra details and the trench that we know and love was born.

Features of the original trench coat could include: wrist straps to keep the wind out; double breasted fastenings; a belt; storm patches for covering the neck more securely; gun pads at the shoulder; epaulettes for holding gloves and folding service caps; and D-rings on the belt to secure grenades, side-arms, and swords. The coat's inherent cool factor comes largely from Hollywood. Characters such as Sam Spade (*The Maltese Falcon*), Rick Blaine (*Casablanca*), and Inspector Clouseau (*The Pink Panther*) made sure that the trench maintained a high public profile throughout the 20th century. Humphrey Bogart is thought to embody the trench attitude of jaded cool, despite only wearing the coat in two scenes in *Casablanca*. The trench was in the spotlight again in 2006, when the Anglomania exhibition at the MET in New York was publicly criticized by the PETA animal rights group, who demanded that a fox-trimmed trench coat be removed from display. The piece in question was designed by Christopher Bailey, wunderkind designer at Burberry who continues to reinvent the item for a generation as young as Romeo Beckham, who starred in a recent Burberry campaign.

ROSE BERTIN AND MARIE ANTOINETTE: SHOCKING TRENDS AND LUXURY FASHION

ROSE BERTIN WAS MILLINER and dressmaker to queen Marie Antoinette, and was dubbed her Minister of Fashion. Despite being a "commoner," she was often received at court by the queen—in breach of etiquette—such was the passion that Marie Antoinette had for fashion and expressing herself through dress. Bertin was hugely influential over the trends of the French court, due to her proximity to and influence over the queen. Marie Antoinette—criticized for the flamboyance of her dress—was never able to strike the right balance between clothing that was appropriate for monarchy while not demonstrating excessive opulence in a land that was increasingly economically divided. In the early 1780s, encouraged by Rose Bertin, Marie Antoinette took up a simpler, faux-rural mode of dress when at Petit Trianon, her country retreat in the grounds of the Palace of Versailles. The look consisted of loose muslin dresses, worn without panniers so the soft fabric could—shockingly—mold to the shape of the legs. A portrait in this style caused moral outrage across the country. The dress was so light and flimsy it was believed she had been painted in her underwear, and it quickly garnered the moniker "chemise a la reine." Not only was this scandalous in itself, but she was also accused of lacking patriotism. The swathes of muslin—imported from India—led to accusations that she was putting French silk merchants out of business. Marie Antoinette eventually reverted to the elaborate court styles, where Bertin's opulent creations became symbolic of the imbalance of wealth of the Ancien Régime. While people starved and revolution drew closer, pamphleteers denounced Bertin as a "corrupt and corrupting maker of luxury goods." Marie Antoinette—herself a symbol of the excesses of aristocracy—was guillotined in 1793. Rose Bertin fled to London to avoid the Terror, and only returned to France in 1795, by which time the upheaval had irrevocably changed fashion and paved the way for more egalitarian styles to gain favor.

HOW TO . . . TIE A WINDSOR KNOT

1 Keep the thick end of the tie on your right and extend it about 30 cm below the other end.

4 Pull it down through the loop and around the thin end.

2 Cross the thick end over the thin end and bring it up through the loop.

5 Turn it and pass it up through the loop.

3 Bring the thick end behind the thin end and up on the right.

6 Bring it down through the front loop, tighten to fit and straighten.

TAILORING: APPRENTICESHIP AND GUILDS

SAVILE ROW HAS BEEN SYNONYMOUS with London style and the epitome of smart men's dressing for two centuries, but the craft associated with the business dates back much further. The Merchant Taylors' Company was formed by the 14th century and made up one of the Twelve Great Livery Companies who emerged from the Medieval Guild system with significant power and financial wealth by the 16th century.

For nearly 300 years from the mid-1500s the apprenticeship system was regulated by law; it was forbidden to practice a craft without having served a period of time under a Master Craftsman. While it's no longer governed by legislation, the apprenticeship system is still the recognized means of entry to Savile Row. Pre-apprenticeship courses are taught at Newham College in conjunction with the Savile Row Bespoke Association, and The Golden Shears prize is awarded biennially to the best emerging tailor, sponsored by the Merchant Taylors' to promote new talent in the field. Under the bespoke sectional system employed at Savile Row it can take up to nine people to create a single garment. Apprenticeships remain the linchpin of this method that produces some of the highest-quality craftsmanship anywhere in the world.

PRINT TERMINOLOGY 1

APPAREL YARD GOODS: In the 18th and 19th centuries, fabric was sold by the piece rather than the bolt, but today wholesale quantities are the norm. Fabrics are printed in continuous lengths and sold by the yard to be sewn into clothing. Apparel yard goods is the term for this, whether it's sold direct to the public (retail) or to "jobbers"—wholesale middlemen for the textile industry.

CALICO: Originally a cotton cloth (the name comes from the Indian city of Calicut), it also came to refer to a very small-scale, brightly colored floral print.

CHINTZ: This originated as a type of cloth, specifically a glazed calico. "Chintz" is the Anglicized plural for the Hindi word "chint," meaning "spotted." Since the 19th century the term has also referred to the print decoration, which is typically a floral on a pale background. These Indian-imported textiles were so popular in 17th- and 18th-century Europe that sumptuary laws were often imposed, banning them in favor of domestic products.

CONVERSATIONAL: A print that features a real creature or object—with the exception of flowers, which are a grouping on their own. This could include photo prints, scenic prints, or characters or objects on a striped or plain background, among many other variations. They are also known as novelty prints as they tend to be used less frequently than other categories of print outside of children's wear. Commemorative and souvenir prints also fall into this category, as do toiles, camouflage, letters and numbers, animal skin prints, and licensed cartoons like Mickey Mouse.

DITSY PRINTS: Small scale repeat prints in a random order (not in stripes or geometric patterns). Most often the subject is florals.

FLORALS: This may sounds obvious, but not all organic matter are considered florals in print terms. All flowers, including grasses and wheat, are grouped as florals. But produce like fruit, vegetables, nuts, or pinecones are considered conversationals. Trees are conversationals, but their leaves are florals. Florals are also somewhat abstract; if they occur in a scenic print it's classified as a conversational. Florals are the most popular category of print.

FOULARD: Originally the word for a lightweight silk cloth in the 19th century which was typically made into block printed handkerchiefs. The name has evolved to refer just to the pattern, which usually consists of small set, evenly spaced geometrics or paisleys (think classic neckties) or could be more architecturally ornate, and bordered with conversationals such as rope or chains (think Celine or Hermes scarves).

REVOLUTIONARY SWIMWEAR

S WIMWEAR company Jantzen started life as a knitting company in Portland, Oregon in 1910. Billed as "The Suit That Changed Bathing to Swimming," their revolutionary one-piece swim-suits actively promoted the physical nature of swimming and clad many a seasoned professional as well as day trippers and coast dwell-ers alike. Always keen to position itself as a fashionable—as well as practical—product, a national US campaign after the First World War saw illustrated adver-tisements appearing in style bibles such as *Vogue* and *Life* as well as on billboards throughout San Francisco and Los Angeles. They were also market leaders when it came to celebrity endorse-ment, from the 1924 Olympics in Paris where both gold (Johnny Weissmuller) and silver (Duke Kahanamoku) 100 meter swimming medalists wore Jantzen, to their catalogs of the '30s that reveled in Hollywood's new fashionable faces, using stars such as Joan Blondell, Dick Powell, and Ginger Rogers to advertise their wares. Always keen to move with the times, Jantzen were quick to associate themselves with other expanding consumer areas. They soon became synony-mous with the growing popularity of motoring through car ornaments and windshield stickers that Jantzen dealers gave away for free. In 1931 the "Shouldaire" swimsuit encour-

aged strap-free tanning, feeding into the outdoor fads of the '30s and the suntanned skin supposedly popularised by Coco Chanel at the Riviera. In the '40s Jantzen added active sportswear to their remit, and in the '50s, with the rise of commercial jet planes and increased leisure time spent at exotic destinations, Jantzen created an "International Set" range for the travel-savvy customer. Jet set fashion at its finest.

VICTORIAN MOURNING CRAZE

IN 1861 ON THE DEATH OF Prince Albert, Queen Victoria was plunged into a state of mourning that would last until her own death 40 years later.

The elaborate rituals of mourning were already in place, but fueled by Royal patronage the business grew ever-more elaborate and the mourning industry thrived. Rules dictating etiquette and clothing were complex, and were laid out in popular women's journals of the day.

The length and depth of mourning depended very much on your relationship to the deceased. Each family member, and even the household servants, went through periods of mourning. For widows the period was two years, for grandparents or siblings six months, through to four weeks for cousins.

For full mourning, Widow's Weeds comprised of a black wardrobe with crape trimmings, but without any additional decoration such as lace. Crape was the fabric of mourning as its dull surface didn't reflect any shine. Non-reflective paramatta silk or bombazine were also used for garments.

On entering half-mourning (generally after the first year and a day), the crape and the white widow's cap could be removed and the color palette could be extended to include chocolate tones, purples, and shaker or silver grays.

Jewelry also had its own set of rules. Whitby jet—a type of fossilized coal—was the ornament of choice for mourning due to its deep black color. This was the only jewelry permitted for full mourning. For half-mourning, hair art could also be worn; intricate rings, brooches, bracelets, or lockets laced with the hair of the deceased—which may sound morbid now but functioned as a tangible reminder of the loved one in an age of high mortality rates.

Mourning was such a lucrative business that entire department stores could be dedicated to providing the right items. From 1841 Jay's Mourning Warehouse of Regent Street was the largest such establishment in London.

The silhouette of mourning clothes had to reflect the fashions of the day, so it could prove to be a very costly procedure indeed. It was only after the horrors of the First World War and the reinvention of black as a color of fashion by designers like Coco Chanel that such elaborate mourning customs generally fell out of favor.

"I think there is beauty in everything. What 'normal' people would perceive as ugly, I can usually see something of beauty in it." ALEXANDER MCQUEEN

BEHIND THE SEAMS: FASHION DOCUMENTARIES 1

VALENTINO: THE LAST EMPEROR (Dir. Matt Tyrnauer, 2008): Directed by a special correspondent for *Vanity Fair*, this documents the working life of one of the behemoths of Italian fashion, with an emphasis on his relationship with companion and business partner Giancarlo Giammetti.

THE SEPTEMBER ISSUE (Dir. R.J. Cutler, 2009): Grace Coddington was little-known outside of fashion inner circles until this documentary catapulted her to household name-fame. An insider's sneak peek into the process of putting together the biggest annual edition of the world's best-known fashion bible.

A MAN'S STORY (Dir. Varon Bonicos, 2010): Director Bonicos followed British designer Ozwald Boateng for 12 years. The result is a film following his highs and lows, from his store on Savile Row to becoming creative director at Givenchy.

LAGERFELD CONFIDENTIAL (Dir. Rodolphe Marconi, 2007): An in-depth look into the regimented life of one of the most outspoken men in fashion. Notoriously private, Lagerfeld remains somewhat aloof, and yet his elaborately constructed persona makes for compelling viewing.

VERSAILLES '73: AMERICAN RUNWAY REVOLUTION (Dir. Deborah Riley Draper, 2012): Documenting a pivotal moment in fashion history, Versailles '73 chronicles the moment that five giants of French fashion were pitted against their American counterparts in a display that challenged notions of race as well as style within the industry.

UNZIPPED (Dir. Douglas Keeve, 1995): Taking us through the story of Isaac Mizrahi's autumn 1994 collection, *Unzipped* covers his inspirations and supermodel friends all filtered through Mizrahi's theatrical style. The success of the film led to him putting together a one-man show, the amusingly titled "Les MiZrahi."

THE TENTS (Dir. James Belzer, 2012): The first comprehensive behind-the-scenes look at New York fashion week from its beginnings in the early 1990s to the powerhouse it is today.

FASHION VICTIM: THE KILLING OF GIANNI VERSACE (Dir. James Kent, 2001): Featuring interviews with family and friends of both victim and killer, *Fashion Victim: The Killing of Gianni Versace* documents the story of Versace's life as well as the events leading up to his death outside his Miami home in 1997.

RENAISSANCE WOMAN

MIUCCIA PRADA IS A FASHION BEHEMOTH, but she hasn't always been involved in the industry. She studied for a PhD in Political Science before spending five years in her 20s training to becoming a mime. After a stint as a Communist Party activist she eventually entered the family business in the late 1970s. Along with her husband and business partner she established the Fondazione Prada in 1995, whose aim is to showcase radical and intellectual contemporary art. Back to the family business, in 1913 her grandfather opened a luxury store in Milan, specializing in leather good such as trunks, beauty cases, and handbags. Just six years later they were supplying the Italian royal family. It wasn't until much later, under the creative direction of Miuccia, that the company moved into clothing, holding their first womenswear fashion show in Milan in 1988. The secondary line, Miu Miu—often referred to as Prada's younger sister—was launched five years later. Prada is arguably the most influential brand of the contemporary fashion landscape—everything Miuccia touches turns to high street trend. Whether she's turning her hand to neoprene or questioning "sweetness" in fashion, her cerebral approach never fails to get fashion editors buzzing.

UTILITY CLOTHING

"MAKE DO AND MEND" became the mantra of World War II, but new clothing was also manufactured throughout the 1940s. The Utility Clothing Scheme was a rationing system that went into effect in 1941 as many textiles were put towards the war effort, so it was imperative that fabric used in clothing was kept to a minimum. The CC41 label was launched, the CC standing for "Civilian Clothing." The following year restrictions were put in place for design details to conserve materials. Dresses were allowed a maximum of two pockets and four meters of stitching. The turn up on men's trousers was banned, and the waistcoat was abandoned, turning suits from three-piece into two-piece. No unnecessary ornamentation was allowed. In order to "glam up" the rather austere designs, couturiers from the Incorporated Society of London Fashion Designers were commissioned to design Utility pieces, including dressmakers-to-the-Queen Norman Hartnell and Hardy Amies, to add a veneer of courtly style. Even though the war ended in 1945, clothes rationing continued until the end of the decade.

> *"Style is a simple way of saying complicated things."*
> JEAN COCTEAU

UNDERWEAR GLOSSARY

BUSTLE: A device for extending the skirt at the back. Materials used have ranged from horse hair pads to fox tails and wire cages. Term "bustle" first used c.1830. Variants worn from 14th–19th century.

BUSTIER: Corset-like garment that only extends to the waist and may include breast-support.

CORSET, EARLIER KNOWN AS STAYS: Worn from below the bust reaching down over the hips, stiffened with whalebone or steel. Fastened with lacing. Used generally to support or mold the figure. From 14th–20th century.

CRINOLINE: Steel springs forming a hoop-like cage which replaced the use of multiple layers of petticoats in the mid-19th century.

FARTHINGALE: A single hoop fastened at the waist by tapes; or a cushion stuffed with hair. Both worn around the waist to extend the skirt. 16th and 17th centuries.

GARTER: A tie or band to keep stockings in place on the legs. May be above or below the knee, depending on historical period.

GIRDLE: Foundation-wear that encases the lower torso extending down, possibly over the hips.

HOSIERY: Today refers to tights. From hose—knitted or woven coverings for the lower leg, an earlier form of stockings.

PANNIERS: Wire, straw, whalebone, cane, or wicker structure worn under the skirt and used to extend the hips sideways. Usually 18th century.

MILITARY CHIC

MILITARY TRENDS CROP UP EVERY SEASON on the catwalk, but the practice of adopting uniform into women's fashion actually stretches back centuries. Dating from 15th-century Hungary, the Hussars had richly colored red uniforms with much gold embroidery and braiding. By the 19th century many European armies had Hussar regiments and with such a decorative aesthetic it's not surprising that women's designs soon absorbed these elements into their dress. Regency women living through the Napoleonic wars were soon wearing braided dolman jackets and pelisse coats—items borrowed from the Hussar's uniform. The Zouave jacket was another popular example. Zouave soldiers were initially the infantry regiments in the French army which were first raised in Algeria in 1831. Again, the term—and uniform—spread and many Zouave regiments fought in the American Civil War. Inspired by North African ornamentation, the original uniform was usually blue or black with elaborate red braiding, and it often included a fez, reflecting the North African origins. The Zouave jacket became a popular women's item for decades, especially after the Crimean War in the 1850s.

FASHION TUNES

WHETHER YOU'RE GETTING READY for a night out or making a playlist for a fashion show, these are some of the audio style essentials from all eras.

TOP HAT, WHITE TIE AND TAILS—Fred Astaire
MINK SCHMINK—Eartha Kitt
ARE YOU HEP TO THE JIVE? (YAS, YAS)—Cab Calloway
FASHION—David Bowie
LOSIN' CONTROL—Fashionettes
LE FREAK—Chic
BLUE JEAN BOP—Gene Vincent
DEDICATED FOLLOWER OF FASHION—The Kinks
DRESS—PJ Harvey
DRESSED IN BLACK—Gossip
SOPHISTICATED BOOM BOOM—Shangri-Las
CUFF LINKS AND A TIE CLIP—Nancy Sinatra
I'M HIP—Blossom Dearie
BLACK SLACKS—Joe Bennett & The Sparkletones
VOGUE—Madonna

·············· A POTTED HISTORY OF SAVILE ROW ··············

1327: A Royal Charter was granted to the livery group who would become the Guild of Merchant Taylors (now the Merchant Taylors' Company).

1689: The tailoring house known as Ede and Ravenscroft is established; they are granted the Royal Warrant as robe makers from King George III to the present Queen. In 1921 it is given its current name, and it remains the oldest surviving family-owned tailoring firm in the UK.

1733: The papers report on a new erection of buildings by the Earl of Burlington, to be named Savile Street (later Row), after his wife, Lady Dorothy Savile.

1760: Thomas Hawkes (eventually of Gieves & Hawkes) arrives in London and is employed as a journeyman (a runner) for a velvet cap-maker on Swallow Street. Having charmed an aristocratic clientele, in 1771 Hawkes opens his eponymous tailoring shop where he dresses both King George III and his son the Prince Regent.

1811: The Prince of Wales becomes Prince Regent, and begins to cut ties with his former favorite, Beau Brummell. Regency dandy Beau Brummell was at the pinnacle of his fame in the years preceding this, and his influence as sartorial advisor to the Prince (later King George IV) had been immense. His tailors of choice are military specialists, Schweitzer on Cork Street and Meyer on Conduit Street. Brummell is largely credited with inventing the suit through his developments, especially through his preference for trousers over knee length breeches. His pared-down style—the antithesis of pre-Revolution French court fashion—focused on black, navy, and buff, with fine cravats of starched linen. People are said to have gone to his townhouse just to see his ritual of washing (which was not generally a daily occurrence at this time) and dressing.

1846: Henry Poole & Company at No. 32 Savile Row is founded, making Henry the "Founder of Savile Row." Later in the century they clothe famous actress Lily Langtry in her riding habits, as well as creating the liveries for her servants.

1849: H. Huntsman & Sons, specializing in riding and sporting clothes, is opened by Henry Huntsman. Queen Victoria and Prince Albert become customers, soon followed by many European Royal houses.

1850: James Lock & Co (who have operated since 1676) develop a Savile Row icon: the bowler hat.

1882: Kilgour is established, who, when merged with French & Stanbury, would go on to conquer Hollywood, including Fred Astaire's 1934 white tie and tails in *Top Hat*, and Cary Grant's sharp suits in Hitchcock's *North by Northwest*.

1902: King Edward VII is crowned and becomes the newest Royal Warrant for the largest establishment on Savile Row, Henry Poole, adding his name to a list that includes the Crown Prince of Prussia, the King of The Belgians, the Khedive of Egypt, Tsar Alexander II of Russia, King Umberto I of Italy, and the Emperor of Mexico.

1912: Hawkes & Co move to No. 1 Savile Row (later Gieves and Hawkes when the two long-standing companies merge in 1974). They go on to become the first company to offer ready-to-wear suits.

1913: Anderson & Sheppard open at No. 13 Savile Row.

1919: H. Huntsman & Sons move to its present address at No. 11 Savile Row.

1921: Rudolph Valentino stars in *The Sheik*, propelling him to worldwide fame. The first Hollywood star to bring his patronage to Savile Row, he sets a trend for future male stars and extends the prestige of London tailoring for a new generation. His prefered firm, Anderson & Sheppard, are also the choice for suit enthusiasts Marlene Dietrich and Katherine Hepburn in the early 1930s.

1946: Couturier Hardy Amies moves in to 14 Savile Row. In 1961 he marks a turning point in men's fashion when he stages one of the earliest menswear catwalk shows at the Ritz.

1969: A new era dawns on Savile Row with the opening of Nutters of Savile Row by eccentric salesman Tommy Nutter and tailor Edward Sexton. They usher in the 1970s with wide legs and lapels, and brash colors. With a client book ranging from the aristocracy to rock stars, Edward Sexton also dresses iconic women in suits such as Bianca Jagger, Yoko Ono, and Twiggy. They also revolutionize retail on the Row, as the first establishment to pioneer "open windows."

1984: Alexander McQueen serves two years of an apprenticeship at Anderson & Sheppard.

1992: Richard James opens, the first of the "New Establishment" tailors. In an attempt to modernize, James brings in Saturday opening and an emphasis on fashion—with an eye on the catwalks—as well as tradition, maintaining techniques, and using British mills. Bryan Ferry and David

Beckham are customers. Another proponent of New Establishment bespoke, Timothy Everest, had been operating from the East End since the late '80s, providing Savile Row-quality casual wear including a bespoke denim service.

1995: At just 28, Ozwald Boateng—another New Establishment proponent mentored by Tommy Nutter—opens on Vigo Street (the south end of Savile Row). Championing bright color and print, he moved to Savile Row proper in 2002 and was the subject of a retrospective at the V&A in 2005.

2004: The Savile Row Bespoke Association is formed to maintain the high production standards and impeccable craftsmanship associated with the bespoke tailoring of the Row. Their label can be found in their members garments from the traditional (such as Gieves & Hawkes, Huntsman, and Henry Poole) to the modern (Chittleborough & Morgan) and New Establishment (Richard James).

2012: Reports that American casual-wear company Abercrombie & Fitch plan to open on Savile Row are met with protest from both tailors and tailoring fans alike.

"Whoever said that money can't buy happiness, simply didn't know where to go shopping." BO DEREK

FASHION ON FILM 1

ROBERTA (DIR. WILLIAM A. SEITER, 1935): Fred Astaire and Ginger Rogers dance their way through the pitfalls of running a Parisian-style couture business.

PRET A PORTER (DIR. ROBERT ALTMAN, 1994): Robert Altman's wry take on the fashion industry, including cameos from supermodels and superstar designers from Naomi Campbell to Jean Paul Gaultier.

QUI ÊTES-VOUS, POLLY MAGGOO? (DIR. WILLIAM KLEIN, 1966): This stylish French art house film spoofs the excesses of the fashion industry while creating a suitably chic monochrome look that has become an inspiration in itself.

FUNNY FACE (DIR. STANLEY DONEN, 1957): Audrey Hepburn learns that you can have brains as well as beauty as Fred Astaire persuades her to leave her job at a bookstore to become a model in Paris.

THE DEVIL WEARS PRADA (DIR. DAVID FRANKEL, 2006): Responsible for putting cerulean blue back into the fashion lexicon, Meryl Streep plays a dictatorial fashion editor believed to be based on *Vogue*'s Anna Wintour.

THE WOMEN (DIR. GEORGE CUKOR, 1939): Nars' Jungle Red nail polish started life here as a key plot device involving gossip at a beauty salon. With Joan Crawford as the ultimate clotheshorse shop girl, George Cukor's classic also features an extended fashion show sequence filmed in glorious Technicolor.

ANNIE HALL (DIR. WOODY ALLEN, 1977): Diane Keaton sparked trends for women in menswear and remains a fashion icon to this day due to her outfits, which were put together by costume designer Ruth Morley and Keaton herself, with a dash of help from Ralph Lauren.

COVER GIRL

KATE MOSS MAY BE THE best-known supermodel in the world, but she's only graced the cover of US *Vogue* eight times, which leaves her lagging far behind Jean Shrimpton (20), Veruschka (13), and Lauren Hutton (26).

"Dress shabbily and they remember the dress; dress impeccably and they remember the woman." COCO CHANEL

"What do I think about the way most people dress?
Most people are not something one thinks about."
DIANA VREELAND

HATS OFF TO LANVIN

LANVIN IS ONE OF THE MOST influential shows on the fashion week schedule but few people know that as well as being relevant today, it's also the oldest fashion house in Paris. Jeanne Lanvin worked for a milliner—as Coco Chanel did years later—before setting up her own hat boutique in 1889.

She first began creating clothing for her young daughter, Marie-Blanche, who features along with Jeanne on the house logo. Her clients, impressed with her designs, ordered adult versions for themselves and by 1909 she had launched head first into a fashion empire. Credited with allowing women's fashions to be more childlike, she made her name throughout the 1920s and '30s with her "robes de style," dresses made in rich fabrics such as velvet, chiffon, lace, and taffeta. She also favored simple, but embellished designs, using embroidery, ribbons, and appliqué.

An early lifestyle brand, she soon ventured into interiors, sportswear, fragrance, menswear, fur, and lingerie. During the war, Lanvin stayed open during the German occupation of France. However, she showed her dissent through her designs; an evening dress was named "Liberty" and a day dress was called "Free France."

FASHION'S FINEST FELINE

KARL LAGERFELD IS ONE OF the fashion world's behemoths. When he's not busy designing for Chanel, Fendi, and his own eponymous label, he can be found in the company of his pampered pet cat Choupette.

Choupette may well be the most well-attended feline on the planet: she has two maids, 24-hour medical attention, and she eats pâté and croquettes from Goyard dishes. Wonderfully and purrrfectly decadent.

········· FASHION MEETS ART ·········

WHILE A CONSTANT DEBATE RAGES around the idea of fashion as art (is it too commercial? Can design be considered art?), there can be no doubt that the two have a long interconnected history.

Sonia Delaunay was an earlier pioneer of Orphism—an offshoot of Cubism that led into Abstract art in the early 1900s. With its emphasis on color and shapes it lent itself well to fabric decoration, and Delaunay's geometric, graphic textile designs found favour in the Art Deco craze of the 1920s.

In 1924 Coco Chanel costumed the Ballets Russes production of *Le Train Bleu*. Far from being the only well-known member of the team, it brought together some of the greatest minds of Modernism: masterminded by Diaghilev, written by Jean Cocteau, costumed by Chanel, with a stage curtain painted by Picasso. The "blue train" was the colloquial term for the train that rushed rich English tourists to the Cote d'Azur each season, and the ballet gently mocks the superficiality of Riviera culture. Cocteau's idea was to recreate a series of living picture postcards, so contemporary crazes like sunbathing and snapshots mixed with gymnastics and Cubist-inspired sets to provide a perfectly stylized—and heavily art-inspired—look at 1920s beach life.

As part of her 1938 Circus Collection, Elsa Schiaparelli collaborated with Salvador Dali on the infamous Skeleton Dress, a dress that caused scandal for its apparent bad taste due to the padded "bones" on the outside of the dress that she had created, forming a kind of evening wear exoskeleton. A big proponent of Surrealism in fashion, Schiap and Dali also created a Lobster dress in 1937 (lobsters were already a big theme of Dali's work), a trompe l'oeil Tears dress that gave the illusion that it was torn and peeling, and a hat in the shape of an upside-down shoe.

Moving into the world of Modern art, Yves Saint Laurent turned the 1960s minimalist shift dress into a canvas when he incorporated De Stijl artist Piet Mondrian's graphic blocks of primary colors into his cocktail dresses in the mid-1960s.

More recently, Marc Jacobs at Louis Vuitton has staged a number of collaborations with artists to play with the idea of the traditional Louis Vuitton monogram branding. Stephen Sprouse added his graffiti aesthetic in 2001 (which has since been reprised by the label), while Takashi Murakami followed in 2002 with his superflat aesthetic. Yayoi Kusama was the 2012 artist of choice, with her trademark multi-size dots gracing clothing, accessories, and in-store decor.

TRANSATLANTIC DICTIONARY

Don't get caught out when shopping overseas!

AMERICAN BRITISH	UK BRITISH	MEANING
Stovepipe	Drainpipe	Tight fitting jeans
Sweater	Jumper/pullover	Knitted top
Pants	Trousers	Bifurcated covering for the legs
Underwear/briefs/boxers	Pants	Men's underwear
Vest	Waistcoat	The smallest part of a three piece suit
Vest	Tank top	Knitted sleeveless garment
Tank top	Vest/vest top	Spaghetti strap summer top
Runners/sneakers	Trainers	Sports shoes
Snaps	Poppers	Fastenings on clothing that "snap" or "pop" together instead of buttons

> *"One is never over-dressed or underdressed with a Little Black Dress."* KARL LAGERFELD, *head designer at Chanel since 1983*

YANKEE DOODLE DANDY

T HE MACARONIS WERE A GROUP of Englishmen in the 18th century who adopted a particularly affected style and manner after taking the European Grand Tour—essentially like a gap year for aristocrats. At their peak their style reached such outrageous levels that their towering, powdered wigs, gigantic shoe buckles, and ornately embroidered waistcoats led to them being greatly satirized by contemporary journalists and artists. The popular children's rhyme "Yankee Doodle Dandy" may seem like gibberish to modern ears, but the line "stuck a feather in his cap and called it macaroni" is actually a reference to a supposed lack of sophistication among Americans—the idea that just one feather could turn them into a man of high fashion.

GIRLS ON FILM: A DIRECTORY OF
40 FASHION PHOTOGRAPHERS

IMAGE-MAKING IS ARGUABLY AS IMPORTANT as garment making in the world of fashion; photographers can make or break the career of models and occasionally designers, and their vision can add depth and narrative to the fashion landscape. Emma Bowkett, photo editor at the *Financial Times FT Weekend* magazine, cites Viviane Sassen as her favorite fashion photographer working today: "For me, Viviane Sassen's fashion photography feels new and exciting. With vibrant colors and contrast, models faces often obscured, her images are graphic and sculptured. She creates narratives that are surreal and intriguing." Without further ado, here are 40 Names To Know in fashion photography both past and present.

ALDRIDGE, MILES: The influence of the psychedelic illustrations of 1960s graphic designer Alan Aldridge can be spotted in the flashes of neon and rich lurid colors of his son Miles' photography. Known for creating a filmic aesthetic that often plays with the idea of Stepford Wives, Aldridge's pictures have a graphicly technicolor appeal and have featured in publications such as *Numéro* and *Vogue Italia*.

AVEDON, RICHARD: Well known for breaking the mold of fashion photography in the late 1950s by asking models to move rather than pose with no emotion, American photographer Avedon shot the Paris collections for nearly 40 years, as well as portraits of everyone from Dorothy Parker to Marilyn Monroe. Providing iconic shots for both *Vogue* and *Harper's Bazaar*, in 1992 he became the first staff photographer at the New Yorker. The photographer behind the controversial Calvin Klein advert featuring a 15-year-old Brooke Shields, he also captured many political events from Vietnam war protests to the fall of the Berlin wall. He was the inspiration behind the character "Dick Avery" in the 1957 musical *Funny Face*, played by Fred Astaire. He also contributed stills to the movie, and the co-star was his long-standing muse Audrey Hepburn.

BAILEY, DAVID: Hailing from East London, Bailey is one of the "Terrible Three" (or "Black Trinity" according to Norman Parkinson) of British postwar photography who helped to create and document the "Swinging Sixties." Working as a photographer's assistant to John French after his National Service, Bailey was first contracted by British *Vogue* in 1960 and caused ripples at the publication with his candid 1962 shoot of Jean Shrimpton in New York. He took portraits of everyone who was

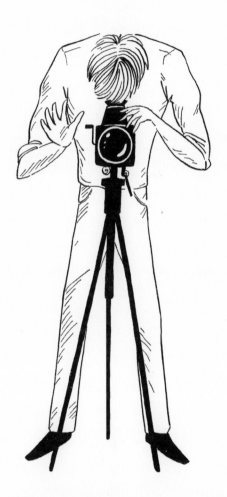

"Fashion is born by small facts, trends, or even politics, never by trying to make little pleats and furbelows, by trinkets, by clothes easy to copy, or by the shortening or lengthening of a skirt." ELSA SCHIAPARELLI

anyone in "Swinging London," from the Rolling Stones to the Kray twins, and the main character in the 1966 Antonioni classic *Blow-Up* was based largely on Bailey, played by David Hemmings. In more recent years he has also directed for film and TV.

BARNOR, JAMES: Born in Ghana in 1929, Barnor became a renowned photojournalist who chronicled the campaign for independence in the 1950s. Seeking further education he moved to the UK to go to art school. When in London he began shooting fashion stories for *Drum* based in Johannesburg; Africa's first black lifestyle magazine. Often set against typical London backdrops such as red post boxes or the recognizable environs of Trafalgar Square, Barnor's photographs are now prized as capturing multicultural life in Britain in the 1960s. Returning to Ghana after ten years, he opened the country's first color-processing lab, before returning again to London two decades later.

BEATON, CECIL: One of the most prolific photographers of the last century, Beaton was also an acclaimed costume and set designer, winning Oscars for his work on *My Fair Lady* and *Gigi*. One of the Bright Young People of the 1920s, his early work was informed by that hedonistic milieu, and he documented many parties and gatherings, on top of his studio work, which was overtly theatrical in tone, paying great attention to set, lighting, staging, and costume. After a swift rise through the fashion press he was fired from American *Vogue* for publishing small, scribbled anti-Semitic phrases alongside sketches in a 1938 edition. He became a war correspondent for the Ministry of Information during the Second World War, where he traveled the globe taking propagandistic images that at times made the conflict look as glamorous as the pre-war parties he had attended. He created some of the best-known images of the 20th century, including the iconic pictures of Queen Elizabeth II on her Coronation Day in 1953. Postwar he also made his name as a theater and film designer, and he remained at the cutting edge of London's social and artistic life throughout the 1960s.

BLUMENFELD, ERWIN: Born in Berlin, Blumenfeld's early work consisted of collages and modified images reminiscent of Dada, a movement he was involved with during his youth in Amsterdam. After a move to Paris in the 1930s, he fled occupied France in 1941 and set up his studio in New York where he was immediately snapped up by *Harper's*

Bazaar. Within a few years he was one of the best known and highly paid fashion photographers in the business. He went on to shoot over 50 *Vogue* covers as well as beauty campaigns for clients such as Dior and Helena Rubenstein. Known for his own distinctive style, he used technology to its fullest, including techniques such as photomontage and solarization to achieve his effects.

BOURDIN, GUY: Although working since the 1950s, Bourdin was at the height of his career from the mid 1970s to the early 1980s, during which time he produced work predominantly for *Vogue* and Charles Jourdan shoes. His images often create a series of dark fantasies concerned with desire and the glamour of consumption with a voyeuristic element verging on fetishism. He has come under criticism for objectifying his subjects, but his distinctive style shifted the boundaries of advertising photography.

DAHL-WOLFE, LOUISE: Setting up her New York studio in 1933, Dahl-Wolfe was shortly hired by *Harper's Bazaar* where she remained as a staff photographer for over 20 years under the formidable fashion direction of Diana Vreeland. A pioneer in the use of color photography, including the juxtaposition of artwork in her portraiture and her use of natural light on location shoots, she is cited as an influence on later photographers such as Richard Avedon and Irving Penn.

DAY, CORINNE: A self-taught photographer, Day broke the mold of fashion photography in the early 1990s through her raw, documentary style dubbed "heroin chic" by the press. A former fashion model, she started her career behind the camera by taking shots of fellow models for their portfolios. She went on to work for publications such as *i-D*, *The Face*, and *Ray Gun* in the early 1990s, where she first worked with a young Kate Moss, capturing some of the earliest images of the future supermodel. As they both found success, Day was chosen to shoot Moss for her first *Vogue* cover in 1993. The resulting spread, shot in Kate Moss' flat, caused an outrage, and was condemned as verging on child pornography; although Moss was 19 she looked considerably younger. Influenced by the documentary art photography of Nan Goldin, Day began documenting the lives of her friends, with an explicit approach that featured sex, drugs, and hardship. She later returned to fashion photography, working for *Vogue* and the National Portrait Gallery.

DEMARCHELIER, PATRICK: French photographer Demarchelier got his start in photography when he was given a camera for his 17th birthday. Living in New York since 1975, he has shot covers for nearly every fashion magazine since the end of the decade including British, Paris, and American *Vogue*, as well as campaigns for luxury companies from Louis Vuitton to Chanel. He has worked closely with *Harper's Bazaar* since 1992.

DE MEYER, BARON ADOLPH: Early fashion photographer Baron de Meyer helped to shape the genre to become an artform of its own. Claiming to have be born in France (though his actual place of birth is unclear), to German and Scottish parents, he joined the Royal Photographic Society in the 1890s and moved to London. The house that he shared with his wife (who was rumored to be the illegitimate daughter of the Prince of Wales) became one of the centers of artistic social life of fin de siècle London and de Meyer's portraits of society people were all the rage. After a move to New York in the early 1910s he turned professional and became the first staff photographer of American *Vogue*. An early pioneer in the field, he made many developments, including the use of backlighting, that would go on to influence future generations.

DONOVAN, TERENCE: Part of the trinity that made up the "'Terrible Three" of celebrity fashion photography in the 1960s, Donovan was part of the social life of "Swinging London." Hailing from East London (along with David Bailey), Donovan was inspired by the industrial, bomb-damaged postwar landscape he grew up with; a far cry from the work of the previous generation of society photographers. He shot his first photo for *Vogue* in 1963 and continued to work for the publication until his death. In the 1970s he also turned his hand to moving image, and went on to shoot commercials and music videos, notably for Robert Palmer's *Addicted to Love* in 1986.

DUFFY, BRIAN: The final link in the "Black Trinity" of 1960s fashion photography, Duffy shot seminal images for Vidal Sassoon as well as the iconic cover for David Bowie's *Aladdin Sane* album, alongside working for all the major fashion publications of the day. Duffy initially studied fashion design, and after leaving Central Saint Martin's College he worked for Victor Stiebel before being offered a job by Balenciaga

that he refused. It was while working as a fashion illustrator for *Harper's Bazaar* that his interest in photography was piqued.

FRENCH, JOHN: Trained as commercial graphic artist, John French set up a photographic studio in 1948. A proponent of the democratization of fashion and the move away from couture in the 1960s, he developed techniques that were suited to printing on cheap newspaper stock and worked regularly for the *Daily Express*. Here he showcased affordable ranges from the emerging designers of the decade to appeal to a teen market. He always had a number of assistants on hand, which included at times both David Bailey and Terence Donovan, who were often in control of triggering the shutter while French focused on details such as set, pose, and lighting. The John French Archive is held at the V&A museum in London.

FRISSELL, TONI: An interest in reportage informed Frissell's work, and throughout her career as staff photographer for *Vogue* in the 1930s, and later for *Harper's Bazaar*, it was the lure of the outdoors, rather than the studio, that inspired her. This was fitting at a time when the rise of sportswear and pared down design was beginning to take hold in American fashion. A short apprenticeship with Cecil Beaton started her career, and during the Second World War she was sent to Europe by the Red Cross to capture life on the home front. On her return to the States she worked for *Harper's Bazaar* and went further afield in her location shoots; this coincided with the postwar economic boom and subsequent rise in international travel which fueled demand for her exotic shots.

HALSMAN, PHILIPPE: Growing up in Latvia, Halsman moved to Paris in the 1920s where he worked for *Vogue*, then fled to New York after the invasion of France during the war. Shortly after arriving in the States, a picture he took of model Connie Ford against an American flag was used in an Elizabeth Arden campaign for "Victory Red" lipstick, which kick started his career on the other side of the Atlantic and led to a cover story in *Life* about women's hats. In the early 1950s he began his "Jump" series; he would ask sitters to jump for a shot at the end of each photography session. He published the collection of "jumpology" in 1959, including such unlikely candidates as Richard Nixon and the Duchess of Windsor. He claimed that in the act of jumping the professional and public mask slipped and you could see the real person. His

37-year collaboration with Salvador Dalí produced some of the greatest Surrealist photos of the 20th century.

HORST P. HORST: Leaving Germany in his youth to study under Le Corbusier in Paris, Horst became assistant to fashion photographer George Hoyningen-Huene. Through the ensuing connections his first picture for *Vogue Paris* was published in 1931. In the late 1930s he met Coco Chanel in New York and went on to photograph her fashions for the next three decades. His prolific career spanned over 60 years; his last picture for British *Vogue* was in 1991. Best known for his classical inspirations and Greek-inspired sets, his photography was mainly studio-based and captured the high glamour of high society.

HOYNINGEN-HUENE, GEORGE: Born into nobility in St Petersburg in 1900, Hoyningen-Huene fled to Britain in 1917 as the revolution was underway. After a move to Paris in the early 1920s he started sketching fashion designs and eventually turned to photography, becoming the head photographer for *Vogue* in 1926. This relationship lasted until 1935, when he moved to the States and signed with *Harper's Bazaar* after reportedly having a falling out with *Vogue*'s art director that almost verged on violent. In 1946 he made the move from New York to Hollywood where he became known for his portraits of film stars and he also worked as a color consultant, set and costume designer. A huge influence on Horst P. Horst (they were reputedly lovers), his photography was also inspired by the statues and sculpture of the classical world.

KLEIN, WILLIAM: Hailed as one of the fathers of street photography, the American Klein trained as a painter and studied at the Sorbonne in the 1940s. It was on a return trip to New York in the early 1950s that he was assigned with capturing the city for *Vogue*; he photographed everyday people on the street at a time when this was rarely done, he even took the step of calling it an ethnographic study. His use of telephoto and wide-angle lenses, high-contrast prints, motion blur, and natural light added to the reportage feel, and the results weren't always embraced by the high glamour fashion industry in his earlier years. His ironic approach was captured in *Who Are You, Polly Maggoo?*—a satirical spin on the world of fashion that he directed in 1966.

KNIGHT, NICK: Multi award-winning photographer Nick Knight published his first book, *Skinheads*, in 1982, which led to a commission from Terry Jones of *i-D* magazine. Throughout his career he has shot for magazines from *Dazed & Confused* to *Vogue*, and ad campaigns for many of the world's top luxury brands from Dior to Jil Sander and Alexander McQueen. He has also directed music videos for Bjork and Lady Gaga. Always at the cutting edge of fashion imagery, Knight challenges traditional concepts of beauty and has said "I don't want to reflect social change—I want to cause social change." From this approach he has tackled many issues that the fashion world often avoids, from racism to disability and ageism. A pioneer of digital fashion, he is the founder and director of SHOWstudio.com, which was set up in 2000 and continues to push boundaries in art and fashion online.

LACHAPELLE, DAVID: Given his first photography job by Andy Warhol when he was 17, LaChapelle has continued Warhol's interest in celebrity and has turned it into a celebration—and sometimes critique—of 21st-century pop culture. His hyper-real images in garish colors often reference art history and play with themes of glamour, consumption, and surrealism, epitomized by a 1995 shot of Lil Kim naked except for the Louis Vuitton monogram painted all over her body. A self-confessed fusion of commercial and fine art photography, he has also directed music videos and documentaries, and he took the last picture of Andy Warhol before he died. Focusing on his fine art photography, and reportedly frustrated with the "divas" of the pop world, LaChapelle officially retired from fashion photography in 2006.

LATEGAN, BARRY: Lategan's biggest contribution to the history of fashion was his early discovery of Twiggy; following his shots of her the *Daily Express* named her the "Face" of 1966 and some of the pictures are held in the archives of the V&A museum. It was through photographing Grace Coddington—when she was model rather than art director—that Lategan got his first foray into British *Vogue*, where his fashion editorials captured the spirit of the age in the 1960s and 1970s.

MAN RAY: The avant-garde photographs of Man Ray span the traditions of Dada and Surrealism, and he was an early pioneer of photography as high art. Hailing from Brooklyn, New York, Man Ray moved to the artist's region of Montparnasse in Paris in the early 1920s, where

he captured members of the bohemian elite from Gertrude Stein to Jean Cocteau, and his work was included in the first Surrealist show in 1925. While his photography was steeped in artistic traditions, he also worked for publications such as *Harper's Bazaar*, *Vogue*, and *Vanity Fair* where he shot garments by many of the leading couturiers of the 1920s and 1930s such as Poiret, Lanvin, Vionnet, and Schiaparelli. This financed his more experimental work where he played with techniques such as solarization and "Rayographs"—photographic images produced without a camera.

MEISEL, STEVEN: Having initially studied illustration, early in his career Meisel worked as an illustrator for designer Halston and trade bible *Women's Wear Daily*. Since his transition to photography he has become one of the most influential fashion photographers working today, and has launched the careers of many models. He has a long-standing relationship with *Vogue Italia* (since 1988) for whom he currently shoots every cover. His worked gained notoriety in 1992 after he photographed Madonna for her book *Sex*; three years later he was again surrounded by scandal when a campaign for Calvin Klein Jeans ended with an FBI investigation into the age of the models. Meisel has often courted controversy through his editorial shoots, such as a 2006 shoot focusing on post 9/11 civil liberties, and an oil slick shoot in the wake of the Gulf of Mexico oil spill, both for *Vogue Italia*. While Meisel has stated the importance of opening a dialog with these areas, others have criticized him for capitalizing on sensitive social issues. He shoots for many major fashion houses, including the coveted Prada campaign, which he has shot since 2004.

MERT AND MARCUS: Collectively inspired by the work of Guy Bourdin and Helmut Newton, Mert Alas and Marcus Piggott have been working together since the mid 1990s when their first collaborative endeavor made the cover of *Dazed & Confused*. Known for their highly stylized portraits and use of digital manipulation resulting in flawless skin and bodies in saturated color or chiaroscuro mono-chrome, their work has been hugely influential on the development and aesthetic of contemporary fashion photography. Their strong yet glamorous images that verge on artificiality have made them a favorite with high-gloss commercial brands, from Roberto Cavalli to Versace and Gucci.

MILLER, LEE: Initially a model, Lee Miller's career started off on the cover of American *Vogue*. In 1929 she moved from the States to Paris and sought out the photographer Man Ray. She became his muse and apprentice, and began contributing her own work to Paris *Vogue*. During the Second World War she was a prolific contributor to British *Vogue*, where she covered all areas from fashion to photojournalism, and she soon became their war correspondent, covering events such as the Liberation of Paris and the Dachau concentration camp.

MOON, SARAH: Initially working as a model, Marielle Hadengue changed her name to Sarah Moon and turned to photography in the 1970s. She went on to become the first woman to shoot the Pirelli calendar in 1972. She worked closely with Barbara Hulanicki of the famed Biba boutiques, shooting their mail order catalogs and helping to establish the aesthetic of the brand. She shot for Cacharel for two decades, and she also lends her romantic aesthetic to fashion's more leftfield brands such as Issey Miyake, Sonia Rykiel, and Comme des Garçons.

NEWTON, HELMUT: born in Berlin to Jewish parents, Newton's family fled the country amid rising anti-Semitism in the late 1930s, ending up in Australia. After establishing a photography company Newton secured a commission from British *Vogue* in 1956. He moved to London then Paris where he shot for all the major fashion magazines as well as more risqué titles such as *Playboy*. His much-imitated style was known for its erotic content, often featuring sadomasochistic overtones that earned him the nickname King of Kink. He developed a neo-noir aesthetic with themes reminiscent of his childhood in Weimar Berlin. At times he was criticized for objectifying his sitters, but the women in his images were anything but passive and were often styled as Amazonian dominatrix. His style lent itself to the louche and slightly controversial, such as the campaign for Yves Saint Laurent's Le Smoking tuxedo for women in the early 1970s.

PARKINSON, NORMAN: One of the best-known fashion photographers of the 20th century, Parkinson was active from the 1930s through to his death in 1990, a career which included working variously on staff at *Vogue*, *Queen*, and *Harper's Bazaar*. He became the official royal photographer in 1975 and as he progressed his style adapted with the times; his pictures always looked fresh rather than dated. Famed for his dapper appearance of curled mustache and trademark embroidered hats, he was also known for his somewhat eccentric behavior that included setting up a pig farm in Tobago from where he supplied his Famous Porkinsons Bangers to the likes of Concorde and the Ritz.

PENN, IRVING: Hailing from New Jersey, Penn started at *Vogue* in the 1940s and worked for the magazine for seven decades. His career at the publication was so prolific that Anna Wintour dedicated the entire July 2007 issue of American *Vogue* to Penn, in honor of his 90th birthday. He was best known for his fashion work, but his repertoire also borrowed from traditions of ethnography and Modernist still-life portraits of found objects. His images had a classic quality that meant his style didn't date over the decades, so much so that he remains the longest serving photographer at *Vogue* in the history of Condé Nast. In 1990 the National Portrait Gallery and the Smithsonian American Art Museum jointly acquired an array of his finest images.

RANKIN: It was while studying at London College of Printing that John Rankin Waddell met Jefferson Hack with whom he founded cutting edge magazine *Dazed & Confused* in 1992. The subsequent publishing empire has gone on to launch *AnOther Magazine* (2001) and *AnOther Man* (2005), as well as dazeddigital.com. Rankin's work often plays with aesthetic ideals; leading from this he shoots the Dove "real women" campaign that aims to extend society's view of beauty. Interested in the democratization of the image, in 2009 he launched Rankin Live: an interactive exhibition where he photographed members of the public—one every 15 minutes—with the aim of proving that anyone can look like a cover star. He has presented photography documentaries on subjects such as South African photography and the story of *Life* magazine, and is also a prolific music video director.

RICHARDSON, TERRY: Raised in Hollywood, Richardson's work is notorious for its explicit nature and raw aesthetic, a look he has been known to achieve using instant cameras and stark lighting. An anti-glamour look, he often places celebrities or models in mundane situations, contrasting with their star status. The sexual nature of many of his photos has caused controversy both in the reception of the images and on occasion during the shoots themselves, and allegations of exploitation and sexual misconduct have at times been levied. His

edgy imagery is regularly used by high profile luxury brands such as Miu Miu, Gucci, and Mercedes-Benz.

RITTS, HERB: The graphic black-and-white simplicity of Ritts' imagery served to mythologize celebrities throughout the 1980s and 1990s. Inspired by Greek sculpture, his emphasis on the human form served the body-conscious fashions of the time well and as such he was a contributor to *Vogue* for over 15 years. During this time he fanned the flames of the supermodel craze through his iconic group shot of Stephanie Seymour, Cindy Crawford, Christy Turlington, Tatjana Patitz, and Naomi Campbell naked in Hollywood in 1989. He also worked with the biggest pop stars of the day, making music videos for such luminaries as Madonna, Mariah Carey, and Michael Jackson.

SNOWDON: Working as a photographer for over 50 years, Anthony Armstrong-Jones was educated at Eton and Cambridge where he studied architecture. On taking up photography after university Snowdon became known for his royal portraits, and throughout his career has shot everyone from Barbara Cartland to Damien Hirst and Laurence Olivier. He was given his title—the 1st Earl of Snowdon—on marrying Princess Margaret (the Queen's sister) in 1960 in respect of his Welsh roots, amidst concerns over the potential for a royal child to be born without a title. The marriage was largely unhappy; as members of the party-loving celebrity set of 1960s London there were rumors of infidelity on both sides and Snowdon is known to have fathered children outside of his marriages as well as within them. In 2012 he collaborated with Acne on a book called *Snowdon Blue*, which demonstrated his predilection for asking sitters to pose in a utilitarian blue shirt. Acne published the book and designed a range of shirts inspired by the images.

SORRENTI, MARIO: Best known for his nude spreads in *Vogue* and *Harper's Bazaar*, Sorrenti was born in Naples and bred in New York. Working as a model in his youth, he shot to fame as a photographer in 1993 at the age of 21 with pictures of his then-girlfriend Kate Moss for the Calvin Klein *Obsession* perfume campaign. The self-taught photographer has since produced campaigns for leading luxury brands from Yves Saint Laurent to Prada.

STEICHEN, EDWARD: In 1911 Steichen shot the latest collection of couturier Poiret for the magazine *Art et Décoration*, which is now generally regarded as the first ever fashion shoot. He was affiliated with many of the art photography societies of the early 20th century and made many advances in the field throughout his lifetime. In 1923 he became chief photographer for *Vanity Fair* after a meeting with publisher Condé Nast, a position he held until 1937 and which also included regular work for *Vogue* where his studio shots traversed the boundaries between art and commercial photography. He served through both world wars; the aerial photography he undertook during the First World War greatly influenced his style and moved him toward a modernist, geometric aesthetic as opposed to the pictorialist, soft-focus style of his former years. Postwar he held the position of Director of the Department of Photography at the Museum of Modern Art in New York until 1962.

TELLER, JUERGEN: A raw, documentary style with flash lighting has become a trademark for German photographer Juergen Teller. Best known for shooting the—sometimes provocative—Marc Jacobs campaigns since 1998, he has also worked for brands such as Helmut Lang, Vivienne Westwood (the woman and the label), and Yves Saint Laurent. Starting out with music, his image of Sinead O'Connor for the single *Nothing Compares 2 You* brought him recognition and his work has appeared in style magazines since the late 1980s, bringing a fresh look to fashion photography that was the antithesis of the highly-polished work of many of the image-makers at the time.

TESTINO, MARIO: One of the highest profile fashion photographers working today, Testino is regularly booked for the biggest, glitziest brands around from Burberry and Gucci to Dolce & Gabbana and Versace. Born in Lima, Peru, he moved to London in the late 1970s, but it was his work styled by Carine Roitfeld (later of French *Vogue*) in the early 1990s that initially got him noticed. As a team they worked on the Gucci campaign and Testino's glossy aesthetic was set; the images, along with Tom Ford's designs, helped to revive the Gucci brand in the mid-1990s. In quick succession Testino shot Madonna and Princess Diana (just months before she died) making him the celebrity fashion photographer du jour and he has become almost as famous as the faces he photographs. His high gloss, high glamour, brightly colored images

formed a contrast to the photographers who had embraced the heroin chic look in the 1990s. He is credited with turning Gisele Bündchen into a supermodel through his proliferation of images, and he currently shoots the next generation of royals, which included the engagement photo for Prince William and Kate Middleton.

VON UNWERTH, ELLEN: German model-turned-photographer von Unwerth specializes in erotic femininity. She worked as a model for a decade before switching to the other side of the camera, where she was credited with launching the career of Claudia Schiffer through a campaign for Guess in the 1990s. There are hints at S&M practices running through her work, inspired by Bettie Page and a notion of strong feminine sexuality. She has directed music videos for Duran Duran among others and has also shot top pop stars of the day from Britney and Christina to Beyoncé.

WALKER, TIM: Regularly working with renowned stage designers and prop builders such as Shona Heath and Rhea Thierstein, Walker's photography creates a magical world full of giant dolls, Humpty Dumpties and anthropomorphized insects. Subsequent to his graduation in 1994, Walker worked as assistant to Richard Avedon before shooting his first story for *Vogue* at the age of just 25. The theatrical staging and styling in his work produces a fairy tale aesthetic unlike any other photographer working today, forging beguiling narratives throughout his editorial shoots that have graced the pages of the world's glossiest magazines.

JAMES LAVER'S HEMLINE THEORY

EMINENT DRESS HISTORIAN James Laver came up with some of the first theories relating dress to economy, politics, and society. His hemline theory, first published in 1963, stated that hem length was equated with the boom and bust economy. Hemlines rose in the hedonistic 1920s, only to drop after the 1929 crash and into the Depression of the 1930s. Again they rose in the consumer-driven 1960s, to fall sharply again with the financial troubles of the 1970s. This is seen as somewhat simplistic now, but theories like this laid the foundations for the discipline of Fashion Theory as we know it today.

THE BIRTH OF THE TUXEDO

ACCORDING TO SAVILE ROW tailors Henry Poole & Co, the tuxedo started life as a short evening jacket that was made by Henry Poole for the Prince of Wales (later Edward VII and at the time very much a trend-setter) in 1860, for informal dinner parties. As legend goes, in 1886 an American named James Potter visited London where he was invited to Sandringham by the Prince, and was told he could get a similar short jacket tailored for him. On his return to the States, Potter wore the new jacket to his New York country club, the Tuxedo Park Club, and bang! An icon was born. While James Potter remains a shadowy figure, the connection with Tuxedo Park in New York is likely to be true. Henry Poole & Co have held a Royal Warrant as court tailor since 1869 and remain true to their origins: they only make bespoke suits—no made-to-measure or ready-to-wear—and each suit takes an impressive three fittings and 60 hours to finish. Along with the former king, clients have included Charles Dickens, Winston Churchill, William Randolph Hearst, and more surprisingly, Buffalo Bill.

BEHIND THE SEAMS: FASHION DOCUMENTARIES 2

MARC JACOBS AND LOUIS VUITTON (Dir. Loïc Prigent, 2007): A close look at the creative journey of one of the hardest-working men in the industry. Marc Jacobs designs for luxury label Louis Vuitton as well as his own eponymous label and diffusion line; this film takes us through the process with an emphasis on the art collaborations for which Louis Vuitton are famed.

NOTEBOOK ON CITIES AND CLOTHES (Dir. Wim Wenders, 1989): Following Yohji Yamamoto as he prepares a collection for its Paris show, Wenders also covers more esoteric subjects such as the relationship between film, cities, and fashion, and the nature of photography in a digital age.

CATWALK (Dir. Robert Leacock, 1996): The relationship between designer and model, and between models themselves, is explored in this film that follows supermodel Christy Turlington around the international spring fashion shows in the early 1990s.

THE EYE HAS TO TRAVEL (Dir. Lisa Immordino Vreeland, 2011): Fashion editor at *Vogue* and *Harper's Bazaar*, as well as curator at the Costume Institute at the Met Museum, Diana Vreeland is an iconic figure in fashion history. This documentary shows the journey of her life from a peripatetic childhood in Paris to the upper echelons of the fashion industry, capturing her characteristic wit along the way.

GREAT MASCULINE RENUNCIATION

IN 1930, the psychoanalyst John Flugel coined the term the "Great Masculine Renunciation" to describe the previous 150 years of the history of menswear. Before the late 18th century, aristocratic men wore highly decorative clothing. You only need to look at the Sun King with his red heels or the Macaronis with their towering wigs to appreciate this. But toward the end of the 18th century there was a shift away from such overt "plumage." Some credit it as a backlash to the excesses of the French court after the Revolution, some credit it to the original dandy Beau Brummell in London, but the sartorial tone of men's clothing went down a notch, leaving feathers and silks behind for sober colors and fitted silhouettes. Flugel also characterized this phenomenon as the product of the Industrial Revolution, when industry and diligence, rather than frippery and frivolity, were the order of the day. As Flugel eloquently put it, "Man abandoned his claim to be considered beautiful. He henceforth aimed at being only useful." Still to this day, the ubiquitous suit is our stylistic legacy of the Great Masculine Renunciation.

PRINT TERMINOLOGY 2

GEOMETRICS: Prints that are highly stylized and nonrepresentational. Obvious examples are stripes, dots, and pinwheels. Less obvious are stars, cartouches, and the fleur-de-lis—considered too abstract to be a floral.

GOUACHE ON PAPER: An opaque, water-soluble paint, gouache is a textile designer's traditional medium. The color is flat and saturated, which closely resembles the appearance of textile dyes. Painting a design with gouache is the first step in the production of printed textiles. The pattern is painted in repeat according to the specifications of the manufacturer and the design is then sent to the mill.

INDIENNES: 18th-century European (usually French) prints that imitated Indian chintzes when importing the originals was banned by sumptuary laws.

MOIRE: A form of dyeless printing where cloth (generally silk) is run through rollers that crush a pattern into it to make permanent waves in the way it reflects light. Also known as watered silk, the look can be imitated by conventional printing on any textile.

OMBRE: Colors are distinguished by a gradual fading and blending into each other.

PAISLEY: This motif, also known as the pine, is the subject of heated and contentious debate. Now a ubiquitous print, scholars have found it incredibly difficult to pinpoint its exact genealogy. It's generally agreed that it developed as a stylized plant form in either Persia or India. The proliferation of the print in India in the 17th century led to its popularity in European markets, and emblazoned on Indian cashmere shawls they became a fashion accessory for the very wealthy by 1800—these shawls were said to cost as much as a London townhouse. The English name for the print comes from the town in Scotland that became the foremost producer of British paisley shawls in the first half of the 19th century.

PALAMPORE: Ornate, large-scale, hand-painted cotton panels from India featuring a highly decorated tree. Created using the mordant-dye technique, they were highly valued by Europeans from the 17th century onward. The quest to reproduce these pieces en mass was a driving force behind the industrial revolution.

VOGUE TIMELINE

HISTORY OF A FASHION BIBLE and luxury publishing empire

1892: *Vogue* magazine was founded as a weekly publication in the United States

1914—1951: Edna Woolman Chase is Editor in Chief of American *Vogue*

1916: British *Vogue*

1920: *Vogue Paris*

1932: American *Vogue* used a color photograph on the cover for the first time

1957: *Vogue New Zealand* (stopped circulation 1968)

1959: *Vogue Australia*

1963—1971: Diana Vreeland serves as Editor-in-Chief of American *Vogue*

1965: *Vogue Italia*

1968: *L'Uomo Vogue*

1973: *Vogue Brazil*

1979: *Vogue Germany*

1987: *Vogue Spain*

1988: Anna Wintour became Editor-in-Chief of American *Vogue*

1992: Alexandra Shulman became Editor-in-Chief of British *Vogue*

1996: www.vogue.co.uk launched

1996: *Vogue Korea*

1996: *Vogue Taiwan*

1998: *Vogue Russia*

2000: *Vogue Latin America/Mexico* (*Vogue En Español*)

2000: *Vogue Nippon* (Japan)

2001: *Teen Vogue*

2002: *Vogue Portugal*

2005: *Men's Vogue* founded (stopped circulation in 2008)

2005: *Vogue China*

2007: *Vogue India*

2007: British *Vogue* launched the first women's magazine YouTube channel

2010: *Vogue Turkey*

2012: *Vogue Netherlands*

2013: *Vogue Thailand*

2013: *Vogue Ukraine*

2013: *Miss Vogue* launches with Cara Delevingne gracing its front cover

ABOVE-THE-TABLE DRESSING

THE COSTUME DESIGNER known simply as Adrian dressed the most glamorous stars throughout the Golden Age of Hollywood, and became a celebrity in his own right with his screen credit simply reading "Gowns by Adrian." He is best known for his collaborations with "clothes horse" star Joan Crawford, and especially for inventing her signature wide-shouldered style, which became an enduring fashion silhouette in the 1930s and 1940s. The shoulders made their first appearance in the 1932 film *Letty Lynton*, which has hardly ever been seen since as it was the subject of a copyright trial shortly after it was released. Various fashion designers, such as Schiaparelli, claimed to have kickstarted the wide-shoulder trend, but Adrian certainly popularized the motif for a wider audience. He also became well known for his maxim of "emphasis above the table." Due to the importance of close-ups, Adrian ensured that all eye-catching detail was focused on the top half of the body and predominantly at neck height, so the shoulders, sleeves, and decolletage were areas to which he paid particular attention on his elegant evening gowns. He also designed costumes for *The Wizard of Oz* (1939), including the iconic ruby slippers.

KILLER HEELS

LOUIS XIV—THE SUN KING— could be called the Grandfather of Fashion. His reign saw the birth of the couture industry (the couturieres' trade guild was formed in 1675), and his patronage saw the establishment of the French ballet. Arguably the first fashion advertising also took place at this time, with fledgling couturiers dressing the well-known ballerinas of the day to gain greater exposure. To top all of this, the Sun King also had something of a shoe obsession, especially when it came to red high heels. Red was a costly color to produce—the crimson-colored dye carmine was derived from the cochineal scale insect—and was confined to the nobility of the court, and high heels had yet to garner the associations of femininity that we place on them today. To galvanize his virility to a greater extent, Louis XIV was even known to have battle scenes painted on to some of his shoes. Killer heels indeed.

"Where's the man that could ease a heart like a satin gown?" DOROTHY PARKER

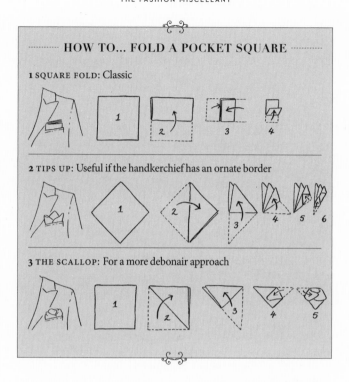

HOW TO... FOLD A POCKET SQUARE

1 SQUARE FOLD: Classic

2 TIPS UP: Useful if the handkerchief has an ornate border

3 THE SCALLOP: For a more debonair approach

CLAIRE McCARDELL: AMERICA'S SWEETHEART

READY-TO-WEAR DESIGNER Claire McCardell has been credited as one of the 20th century's democratizers of fashion. Working mainly between the 1930s to the 1950s, she created affordable, functional, mass-produced womenswear that was also deemed as stylish and "American," as opposed to what was seen as the stuffiness of French couture. She designed for Townley Frocks and also taught at design school Parsons in New York. During the war years, department store Lord and Taylor began an "American Look" campaign, to highlight home-grown design while the fashion capital of France was occupied. McCardell's designs for Townley were heavily promoted through this, and she became one of their best-selling designers. Her Popover dress of 1942 has been especially influential. A wrapover style in a utilitarian denim, it was chic yet practical and, along with many of her other innovations, has been of obvious inspiration to contemporary American designers from Diane von Furstenberg to Calvin Klein.

HAT FACTS

LOCK AND CO. HAVE BEEN fitting hats on royal heads since 1676. Their store on St James Street in London's Mayfair is a hat-lovers heaven consisting of millinery apparatus and artifacts, from a plumed creation owned by Wellington to Victorian instruments for measuring and drawing the head that are still in working order.

During the Edwardian golden age of millinery, ornamentation became ever more elaborate, with elaborate bouquets of flowers, birds, lace, ribbons, bows, feathers and artificial fruit regularly gracing heads of society ladies. Hatpins were essential to secure these creations to the head. These lengthy pins had yet another use in discouraging dangerous advances on the street, so much so that laws were proposed to ban this secret weapon in many cities around the world.

One of our most enduring characters from fiction, Lewis Carroll's Mad Hatter had a grounding in fact. Mercury used in the production of headgear was often inhaled in poorly ventilated workshops, leading to brain damage for a number of unfortunate hatters.

Did you know? Sherlock Holmes doesn't wear a deerstalker in any of the works by Arthur Conan Doyle. It was an addition by his illustrator for one of Holmes' out-of-town mysteries. The association stuck and a hat icon was born!

The Bowler hat has Lock and Co. (see above) to thank for its creation. They commissioned Thomas and William Bowler in 1850 to make a hat suitable for a Norfolk farmer; a hat so sturdy that it was intended to protect gamekeepers' heads from tree branches as they rode around country estates. The practicality of the hat caught on and before long no businessman was fully dressed without one.

During the 1940s the headscarf turban was popular headgear for women working in factories, to stop long Veronica Lake-style hair from getting caught in machinery. The turban of the "Land Girl" symbolized the war effort, patriotism, and utility, as epitomized by Rosie the Riveter.

Out of the factories, hats grew more elaborate during the 1940s as hat-making materials failed to succumb to the strict rationing of many other items of clothing.

The late, great style icon, and fashion editor Isabella Blow is credited with kick-starting the career of milliner Philip Treacy when she let him set up a studio in her flat after his graduation from the Royal College of Art.

From the French word for bell, the cloche hat—which peaked in popularity in the flapper style of the 1920s—symbolized the era's love affair with youth. The over-size hat was worn low on the head to emphasize the young and petite qualities of the wearer. As cars gained in popular-ity, the deep-crowned hats were also less likely to get lost in the wind.

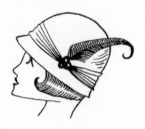

The association of hats with social status has a long lineage. A British sump-tuary law dating from 1571 required every non-noble male over the age of six to wear a wool cap on Sundays and holidays, in an effort to bolster the wool trade. By the time the flat cap became ubiquitous among the Victorian working class, the link between non-nobles and that style of hat had been around for centuries.

Various tales recount the invention of the top hat, from Florence in 1760 to China in 1775. The first recorded wearing of a top hat in London was with haber-dasher John Hetherington in 1797. The oversize hat caused such concern that it is said to have led to near-riots in the streets, and Hetherington was prosecuted for wearing "a tall structure having a shining luster calculated to frighten timid people." It was soon accepted into Victorian society, and was given additional credence from around 1850 when Prince Albert himself adopted the style. They are now seen as symbolic of the industry and progress of the Victorian age—especially through their association with the engineer Isambard Kingdom Brunel and have been likened to the factory chimneys that sprung up through-out the 19th century. The collapsible top hat was developed in 1823 to enable unobstructed opera viewing, and in 1814 the conjuror Louis Comte became the first magician to pull a rabbit out of a top hat.

"You cannot fake chic but you can be chic and fake fur."
KARL LAGERFELD

FASHION ACRONYMS:

Mind your Ps and Qs with our handy guide to fashion parlance

DKO	Designer Knock Off
LBD	Little Black Dress
LSD	Little Sequin Dress
OOTD	Outfit Of The Day
OTK	Over The Knee
RTW	Ready To Wear
TDF	To Die For
VBS	Visible Bra Strap
VPL	Visible Panty Line

"Give a girl the right shoes and she can conquer the world."
MARILYN MONROE

LBD

THE LBD HAS BECOME such a style perennial that it's hard to believe that besides a brief period in the 16th century (when the Spanish predilection for black became all the rage at court), black has not often been seen as a fashionable color for women outside of the dictates of mourning. That all changed in 1926. For the first time American *Vogue* featured a simple black design by Chanel and predicted it would become a "style uniform." At a time when the mass production of Ford's assembly line was revolutionizing car ownership, the straight lines and simplicity of the LBD became Chanel's Model T, with *Vogue* christening it "Chanel's Ford." The look was so pared down compared with what women of fashion were wearing just a decade earlier that it has invited comparison with servant's uniforms, or those of working girls such as shop assistants. Chanel was also fond of telling women to dress "as plainly as your maids." Coupled with the onset of the Great Depression shortly after its inception, the LBD has been seen as a democratizer of fashion despite the discrepancies that come with the designer price tag in Chanel's case, creating a version of "deluxe poor" that is not as egalitarian as the design—or its origins—would lead us to believe.

FASHION WEEK CHECKLIST

IF YOU'RE GOING TO BE BRAVING the shows, you'll need to take the basics: water, camera, notebook, sunglasses. But there are also various items that might not be so memorable. Here Morwenna Ferrier, of *Grazia* magazine, shares her Fashion Week essentials.

1 A BAG OF NUTS. Getting to the canapes is far harder than you'd think. Also, you only want food that can be eaten with one hand as you'll be shaking hands/tweeting/waving/scribbling with the other.

2 WIRELESS PHONE CHARGER. I usually contact people via IM at shows, which devours your battery.

3 A BARBOUR RUCKSACK. Looks a bit scruffy, but carrying swag from show to show will murder your back.

4 A NON-MAN-MADE GARMENT. There's nothing worse than sitting on a cold hard concrete slab for 90 minutes.

5 GRENSON BOOTS—beautiful man boots for women. They have thick rubber soles which double up as wellies, so are perfect for changeable weather.

"Fashion is a form of ugliness so intolerable that we have to alter it every six months." OSCAR WILDE

DEPRESSION-BEATING BANGLES

IN 1909, LEO. H. BAEKELAND developed and created a plastic that once cast could not be melted. From this discovery came the beloved Bakelite jewelry and wares that are now highly collectable and sought after. The popularity of Bakelite was fueled by the Great Depression of the 1930s. Money was scarce and women were searching for an inexpensive way of spicing up their wardrobes. Bakelite was just the answer: unique, fun jewelry in an array of vibrant colors. Those unaffected by the financial downturn also flocked to Bakelite due to one-off designer pieces that could be encrusted with rhinestones and precious metals. Many of these sold for up to thirty dollars, a hefty sum for the time.

"A women with good shoes is never ugly. They are the last touch of elegance." COCO CHANEL

FASHION ON FILM 2

MARIE ANTOINETTE (DIR. SOFIA COPPOLA, 2006): With its Laduree palette, Kirsten Dunst's Marie Antoinette takes the "let them eat cake" mentality to its natural conclusion, despite a less-than-rigorous basis in history.

PANDORA'S BOX (DIR. G. W. PABST, 1929): Louise Brooks continues to inspire bob-envy in generations of silent film lovers in this early femme fatale story, which even features Jack the Ripper at its grisly end.

BREAKFAST AT TIFFANYS (DIR. BLAKE EDWARDS, 1961): Audrey Hepburn as Holly Golightly became a film and fashion icon in a simple Givenchy dress, beehive, oversize cigarette holder and sunglasses.

GILDA (DIR. CHARLES VIDOR, 1946): Rita Hayworth set the benchmark of glamour as the ultimate vamp in the title role of this film noir classic.

THE WILD ONE (DIR. LÁSZLÓ BENEDEK, 1953): Marlon Brando as a smouldering, leather-clad biker gang-leader was considered so subversive that the film was banned in the UK for 14 years. The "delinquent" look of black leather jacket, t-shirt, and blue jeans became a symbol of postwar youth culture.

BLADERUNNER (DIR. RIDLEY SCOTT, 1982): The "future noir" of Scott's sci-fi masterpiece took the sharp-shouldered styles of the 1940s and infused them with a futuristic chic that's been inspiring designers for decades.

BONNIE AND CLYDE (DIR. ARTHUR PENN, 1967): Theadora Van Runkle's costumes of mustard-tone colors and knitwear helped spark the re-interest in 1930s styles that lasted through into the following decade.

THE FIFTH ELEMENT (DIR. LUC BESSON, 1997): The 23rd century as imagined by Jean-Paul Gaultier resulted in science fiction mixed with a comic book aesthetic in this larger-than-life story. Gaultier produced 954 costumes, from the fetish-tinged flight attendants to Milla Jovovich's bandages.

"Like poetry, fashion does not state anything. It merely suggests." KARL LAGERFIELD

STYLE TRIBES: UP CLOSE AND PERSONAL
WITH SUBCULTURE

ZOOTIES AND ZAZOU: In the 1930s and 1940s, African-American identity was becoming stylistically visible through the zoot suit. Worn by popular bandleaders such as Cab Calloway at clubs in Harlem, and influential men including a young Malcolm X, the look was comprised of very wide high-waisted trousers that tapered at the ankle, coupled with a long jacket fitted through the body with exaggerated, cartoon-like shoulders. In 1942 rationing was imposed on the use of wool in America, which overnight labeled the zoot suits an unpatriotic choice. However, the African-Americans and young Mexicans (known as Pachucos) who favored this style had no problem getting these suits made by backstreet tailors. Racial tension exploded one night in June 1943 when white servicemen on leave attacked zoot-suited youths, leading to what has been called the "Zoot Suit Riots" in Los Angeles that subsequently spread across the country. The outbreak of violence goes to show how subversive dress can be. Zazous were the Zootie's French counterparts who had fallen in love with the swinging sounds of the big band leaders in Harlem. They were deeply unpopular in German-occupied Paris, also for flouting the rationing restrictions put on fabric, and a drive by the Nazis to send them to work camps succeeded in killing off this stylistic movement. Listen to: *Are You Hep to the Jive (Yas, Yas)*—Cab Calloway.

BEATNIKS: Possibly the first instance of anti-style, this subculture originated with the Beat Generation writers of Allen Ginsberg and Jack Kerouac in the late 1940s. The first generation were resistant to sartorial embellishment and favored clothing that defied not only current fashions, but all bourgeois notions of respectability in dress. However, the caricature of the Beatnik—a term coined by journalists that fused Beats with the Russian satellite Sputnik thereby linking them to Communism—was much different. Gracing poetry readings and smoky jazz clubs, adorned in black polo necks, berets, and goatee beards, this stereotype merged with the Existentialists on the Parisian Left Bank to form an image that endures to this day in popular culture. Read: *On The Road*—Jack Kerouac.

TEDDY BOYS: After the Second World War, Savile Row tailors—keen to foster nostalgia and national pride—began harking back to the glory days of British empire with neo-Edwardian suits. These featured long, single-breasted jackets that were often trimmed with velvet at the collar, pockets and cuffs, worn with slim trousers and a brocade waistcoat. The idea of the "teenager" emerged at the same time and despite the austerity of the postwar years, young working class men had more disposable income than ever before. They began mixing the "New Edwardian" style of Savile Row with touches from across the Atlantic like western ties and coiffed hair. The media fueled a moral panic about these "delinquents" that sent shivers down the spine of middle England. Teds weren't entirely blame-free; often accessorized with flick knives, they were also a presence at the Notting Hill race riots. There are frequent resurgences of Teddy Boy style both in alternative clubs and on the catwalk. Listen to: *Rock The Joint*—Bill Haley & The Comets.

MODS: If the Teddy Boys favored styles from the past, the Mods were all about the future. They fused hip American cool jazz and rhythm & blues with culture and style from the continent: vespa scooters, coffee bars, Italian-cut three-button suits and French New Wave films. They adopted a restrained form of dress that harked back to the Regency-era dandy Beau Brummell, who believed that true style is all in the details and should never be too flamboyant, the original "less is more" advocate. Like the Teddy Boys, Mod style and culture is regularly revived, from the film *Quadrophenia* in 1979 (which popularized the parka as a badge of Mod identity) to Oasis in the mid 1990s. Read: *Absolute Beginners*—Colin MacInnes.

ROCKERS: Going down in history as the opposition to the Mods, the Rockers generated a tough image through items traditionally associated with working men or the military, like blues jeans and black leather jackets, albeit customized with hand-painted slogans and metal studs. These antisocial clothing choices emphasized their working-class origins, they didn't dress for success like the sharp-suited Mods. The number of Rockers grew throughout 1963, when motorbike enthusiasts at hotspots like London's Ace Cafe were listening to Rock 'n' Roll from America and increasingly from the UK with acts like Billy Fury. The clashes with the Mods at beach towns across the country have been epitomized by the Brighton fight of 1964. The media—knowing that these fights fueled newspaper sales—are said to have had more than a small hand in setting it up and securing their shots. But the underlying tension between the groups showed how important stylistic expression and differentiation had become for the postwar generation. Listen to: *Brand New Cadillac*—Vince Taylor and the Playboys.

HIPPIES: The Baby Boomer coming-of-age generation was defined by the Hippy counterculture of the late 1960s. Folk revival artists like Bob Dylan and Joan Baez harked back to pre-industrial visions of rural life and community. Psychedelic drugs like LSD encouraged an otherworldly interest in color and also advocated the "turn on, tune in, drop out" lifestyle that reached its apogee in the 1967 "Summer of Love" on the west coast of America. In keeping with the alternative, non-"straight" lifestyle, Hippy clothing courted gender-bending aesthetics such as long hair for all, and a predilection for flared jeans and floral motifs. For the first time, second-hand clothing was bought for its style rather than from necessity, paving the way for the vintage mania of recent years. Moving away somewhat from the Free Love hedonism that defined its early days, the Hippy movement became politicized over the Vietnam war protests. Listen to: *Somebody to Love*—Jefferson Airplane.

SKINHEADS: This much misunderstood subculture began as an evolution of Mod style at a time in the late 1960s when the Mod moniker was usurped by mainstream "Swinging London." Its proponents listened to Jamaican ska and rocksteady, and the clothing was stripped back and fused with the style of Jamaican Rude Boys: two-tone suits, white socks, shiny black shoes, and pork pie hats. There was a class consciousness at work in their dress too, adopting elements of manual laborer's clothing such as steel-toe-capped boots and donkey jackets, and the aggressive aesthetic was often matched in their behavior. The style evolved and the politics mutated—by the 1980s some skinheads were becoming associated with neo-fascism. Despite it being the antithesis of the early Skinhead's style and music, the subculture has now become synonymous with racism. Listen to: *Israelites*—Desmond Dekker & The Aces.

GLAM ROCK: With figureheads such as Marc Bolan and David Bowie, the Glam Rock movement was never going to be a shrinking violet. A reaction to the back-to-nature earthy styles that had come to dominate the Hippy movement, from the early 1970s the music and style of glam rock began celebrating artifice in many extravagant forms. Androgynous flamboyance was the order of the day, including platform shoes and metallic space-age-style clothing that could be teamed with feather boas, excessive costume jewelry, and lashings of makeup. This was arguably the first subculture that really questioned the idea of masculinity. Listen to: *Ziggy Stardust*—David Bowie.

PUNK: As the Baby Boomer generation entered their 30s, a new youth revolution was brewing as a backlash to the peace and love mantra of the Hippies. With the economic crisis in the 1970s and growing unemployment, the optimism of the 1960s soon transmuted into a gray nihilism. Punk style, as with its music, was confrontational, aggressive, and unlike anything else that had come before. By the early and mid 1970s, rock music was increasingly dominated by stadium mega groups and the self-indulgent solos of Prog Rock. The counterculture had become part of the establishment and groups of teens across London and New York were ready for something new. Somewhat ironically, this first surfaced as something old. When Malcolm McLaren and Vivienne Westwood opened their first shop, Let it Rock, on the King's Road in 1971 it was at the forefront of the Teddy Boy and Rocker revivals. In 1974 it morphed into Too Fast To Live, Too Young To Die and started incorporating elements of fetish wear, and the following year as it turned into SEX the transformation was complete. The musical home of Punk is generally credited as CBGB's on New York's Bowery Street, which was regularly showcasing musicians like Richard Hell, The Ramones, Patti Smith, and the New York Dolls by 1974. The term "punk" also came from the Big Apple; initially a term of abuse levied at juvenile delinquents, this new breed of disaffected youths were more than happy to reappropriate it for themselves. Malcolm McLaren—familiar with the music of the New York Dolls—put together the Sex Pistols in part to model the designs of Vivienne Westwood. The DIY ethos evident in early Westwood designs was a common feature of Punk, regarding both style and music, and the term bricolage—taking existing items and giving them new meanings by putting them in strange combinations and unorthodox contexts—defines much of what we think of as Punk style, from Rocker influences to neon colors. The media caricature of the Punk was soon born, wearing bin bags and safety pins, but in reality there was a much broader mix of styles from fetishwear to studded leather jackets and old school uniforms. By the late 1980s Punk style had become such a stereotype that mohican-adorned gangs could frequently be found throughout central London ready to pose for pictures with tourists, for a small fee. Despite being co-opted by the media, Punk subculture has had a huge impact on the mix-and-match way that we dress in the 21st century. Listen to: *Oh Bondage, Up Yours*—X-Ray Spex.

NEW ROMANTICS: Arguably more extravagant than the Punks, the religion for the New Romantics was dressing up and going clubbing. With their name taken from the historical references in their dress that harked back to the first Romantics, with billowing Byronesque shirts and pirate styling, the New Romantic look was all about gender-bending flamboyance. The New Romantic subculture hinged around clubs like "Bowie Night" at Gossip's in London's Soho. Only for the truly initiated, it was held on a Tuesday and revolutionized the idea of the "in-crowd" as punters were only allowed in having been vetted by members themselves who were working the door, rather than some disinterested club manager as had often been the case in the past. As attendance grew it migrated to become the Blitz club in Covent Garden. Run by Steve Strange, glamour was the order of the day; dressing up for dressing up's sake. The club was the catwalk and the stage for transformation at a pivotal point in the early 1980s when a whole host of culture industries were taking off, from MTV to the style press of *The Face* and *i-D* that would go on to offer fashion and music on a round-the-clock basis. Listen to: *Fade to Grey*—Visage.

GOTHS: Many people date the start of the Goth subculture to 1982, with the opening of the Batcave club on Dean Street in London's Soho. The Gothic has a long tradition in art and literature, from medieval cathedrals to Horace Walpole, right through to camper additions like the Addams Family. It makes sense that visions of the Gothic should eventually haunt our streets as well. Spectres of the undead, Goths—with their passion for the macaber—splintered out of other groups such as Punks and New Romantics to form their own subculture, which somewhat ironically is still alive and well today. Dress styles favor copious amounts of black combined with elements that could have been left over from Victorian mourning attire: lace, velvet, corsets, and dark purple tones, often mixed with the tougher aesthetic of leather and chains. Makeup also took on a deathly pallor, contrasted with blood-red lips and dark exaggerated eyes. Listen to: *Grimly Fiendish*—The Damned.

CASUALS: In the history of British subculture it's unusual to find one that doesn't have musical taste at its nucleus. But the group activity of choice for the Casuals was that other British obsession: football. Style emerged on the terraces in the late 1970s and early 1980s that reflected a new type of aspirational, Eurocentric dress. British teams were becoming increasingly successful and as fans traveled to away matches on the continent they also used the opportunity for shopping, picking up brands such as Fila, Lacoste, Ellesse, and even Christian Dior. Often labeled as early metrosexuals, the Casuals increased the popularity of designer sportswear in a decade characterized by the branding and logos of excessive and conspicuous capitalism, while fueling a taste for European goods at home.

LOLITA: While the majority of subcultures featured have sprung from the streets of London or New York, the Lolita style is truly Japanese in inception. While not the earliest, or only, Japanese subculture, Lolita style has spread around the world since the mid 1990s, making Harajuku in Tokyo a sartorial street-style destination on a par with—or even superseding—the quirkier locations in London, New York or Berlin. Based on a Japanese take of western Victorian, Rococo-inspired styles with a dash of fairy tale princess, the classic Lolita silhouette is made up of wide skirts with multiple petticoats for volume. There are many different subsections within Lolita. Sweet Lolita has a doll-like aesthetic that favors pastel colors, gingham, knee-high socks and ultra "girly" trimmings such as bows, frilly umbrellas, and soft toys. Gothic Lolitas, who fuse horror with innocence, may favor a darker color palette and motifs such as crosses and skulls. Guro Lolita takes it even further and becomes a living broken doll, complete with bloodstains, wounds, and bandages. Sailor and Pirate Lolitas have a taste for the nautical. Ōji (translates to "Prince") Lolitas cultivate a look based on Victorian boys. Worn by either sex, the style often features shirts with knickerbockers, top hats or baker boy caps. For more on Japanese street style read: *Fruits*—Shoichi Aoki.

NAILING IT

EXTRAVAGANT NAIL ART might seem like a truly 21st-century trend, but magnificent manicures have actually been around for centuries. Women of the Imperial court in China were expected to grow their nails up to 6 inches long, to prove their distance from manual labor. They even wore beautifully-crafted jade nail guards for protection. Nail coloring such as Henna can also be found in ancient civilizations from India to Egypt. It wasn't until the 1920s and 1930s that real advances were made, in an altogether different industry: motoring. The glossy paint used for cars was soon adapted for the fingernails and a new beauty industry was born. In 1927 Max Factor introduced a rosy cream and a white liquid that formed the basis of what became known as the French manicure. Then in 1932 Revlon was founded on a single product—an opaque nail enamel—which saw it become a multimillion dollar company in just 6 years. In 1994 when Uma Thurman wore Chanel's Rouge Noir in *Pulp Fiction* a nail craze was born. Its origins, again, are less glamorous: a makeup artist colored in models' nails with a black marker pen for a pre-show picture, and recreated the color for the catwalk. It flew off shelves and was an instant bestseller.

GENEALOGY OF JEANS

FAR FROM BEING AN ITEM of high fashion, the first jeans were made in the American west for laborers, miners (including gold miners) and later cowboys. The official birthday of jeans is given as 20th May, 1873: the date that tailor Jacob Davis and dry goods merchant Levi Strauss took out a patent on their pants design that used rivets to reinforce the stitching. In 1936 Levi Strauss added the signature red label to the back of jeans so they could be identified at a distance. The oldest surviving pair of jeans dates from 1879. Fast forward to 1996, and enfant terrible designer Alexander McQueen forged yet another denim revolution with the ultra lowrise "bumster." The look remained popular for well over a decade; without McQueen it's safe to say we would never have heard the phrase "muffin top" outside of baking.

ETYMOLOGY OF STYLE

DENIM: From the French "serge de Nîmes" relating to serge from the southern French town of Nîmes, the term originated in the 1690s. The first recorded use of denim to mean "tough cotton cloth" was 1850 in American English. The term "jeans" is said to come from Genoese sailors who wore coarse, long-lasting, indigo-dyed trousers.

DUNGAREES: From dungaree fabric, a coarse calico, which in turn comes from the Hindi dungri—from the name of a village near Mumbai. C.1610

FASHION: From the Latin facio (making or doing), it became facon in Middle French. By 1489 it had evolved into fashion in Middle English and had acquired its contemporary meaning of a current style of dress, and was especially associated with the upper echelons of society.

PYJAMAS: The word pyjama, or pajama, has its roots in the Persian (pāyjāmeh, from pāy ‹leg› and jāmeh ‹garment›). During the British Raj the term was incorporated into English through Hindustani, and referred to "loose trousers tied at the waist" that were worn by Muslim men in India and were appropriated as sleepwear and loungewear by Europeans. Despite cropping up on various catwalks in recent years, in 2012 a commissioner in Louisiana proposed a ban on wearing pyjamas in public, claiming that it is evidence of the dwindling moral fiber of society. This followed a 2010 ban by a UK branch of Tesco on wearing nightwear in which to shop.

STILETTO: From the Italian stilo (dagger), from the 1610s a stiletto was a "short dagger with a thick blade." Its use with regard to shoe heels is largely associated with Roger Vivier, from 1953.

TROUSERS: The etymology of bifurcated clothing has a long history. Proto-Germanic languages of Old English, Old Saxon, and Old Norse all feature words derived from husan (hose, hosa) meaning "covering for the leg." By around 1200 "breeches" (double plural of Old English brec) was in use, meaning "garment for the legs and trunk," which had related words in Old Norse, Dutch, Danish, Old High German, Celtic, and Latin. By the late 16th century "trouzes" had developed from Gaelic or Middle Irish triubhas, meaning "close-fitting shorts." The next incarnation, pantaloons, derived from the Italian Commedia dell'Arte character Pantalone, a greedy and aged Venetian merchant who wore tight, ankle-length trousers as opposed to knee-breeches. These became associated with the Sans-Culottes during the French Revolution, working class republicans who wore full-length trousers to distinguish themselves from the breeches-clad aristocracy. The term pantaloons was subsequently shortened to pants from around 1840 and went on to become the predominant term in American English. Prudish Victorians euphemistically labeled trousers both "unutterables" and "unmentionables," the latter of which had taken on its meaning of underwear by around 1910.

SHOEMAKER TO THE STARS

FERRAGAMO IS ONE OF THE MOST coveted footwear brands on the red carpet. Proving that glamour and technology don't have to be unhappy bedfellows, the company rests on a lineage of innovation. Salvatore Ferragamo was obsessed with making shoes that were both beautiful and comfortable, and while the former came easily, he studied anatomy to gain a greater understanding of how to increase the latter. He used plumb-lines—previously the preserve of architects and engineers—to establish where the most support was needed in the shoe, which he discovered was the arch of the foot. He developed specialist steel shanks that he patented in 1929 and 1958, which kept his shoes very light, but gave added strength, while other shoemakers at the time were using card or leather. The company connection with the film industry also stretches further than the red carpet, right back to the silent era. Ferragamo's career spanned the Golden Age of Hollywood. He forged early links with the Dream Factory; he moved from Italy to the States at a young age and bought the "Hollywood Boot Shop" in Santa Barbara in 1919. The company did so well that he opened a branch in Hollywood where he stayed until 1927, when he returned to Italy and started his own company. His time spent among the glitterati of the silent era certainly paid off, and throughout the rest of his life he was known for his strong ties to Hollywood, which included designing shoes for silver-screen legends such as Mary Pickford, Sophia Loren, Greta Garbo, and of course Audrey Hepburn. In 2006, long after the death of the founder, the company was even awarded the Rodeo Drive Walk of Style Award for its ongoing contributions to the worlds of fashion and cinema.

FASHION PORTMANTEAUS

THERE'S NOTHING THAT THE FASHION media loves more than a portmanteau. Why use one word, when two half-words would suffice?

BOOT-DAL = Part boot, part sandal.

GREIGE = Possibly the original fashion portmanteau, this color was invented by Giorgio Armani to describe his neutral mix of gray and beige.

JEGGINGS = Trompe l'oeil leggings made to look like jeans.

SHACKET = Cross between a shirt and a jacket, lightweight but structured.

SHBOOT = Part shoe, part boot.

SKORTS = A skirt with added bifurcation.

SKROUSERS = Ever worn a skirt over trousers? You have, in fact, been wearing skrousers.

TREGGINGS = Half trousers, half leggings, as popularized by Kate Moss in her collections for Topshop.

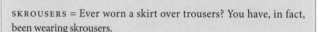

"The best fashion show is definitely on the street. Always has been and always will be." BILL CUNNINGHAM

SPORTING STARS

S PORT AND SARTORIAL FLAIR often go hand in hand. Here are some of history's sports stars who have added their own fair share of panache to the sporting arena.

Suzanne Lenglen was one of the first female sports stars and one of the chicest athletes of the 1920s. A French tennis player, she won many prestigious titles throughout her career, including the Wimbledon singles title, which she won six times in seven years. The majority of her dresses were designed by Jean Patou, and included racy features for the time, such as short sleeves and a short hemline. She was also known for her trademark headgear: a stylish bandeau to keep her hair in place. She was even the inspiration behind one of the characters in a Ballets Russes play penned by Jean Cocteau. In 1930 she became director of the sports department at the Yvonne May couture house, where she capitalized on her look by creating tennis wear in silk with matching jackets and hair bandeaus.

Now synonymous with a number of British subcultures from Northern Soul fans to skinheads, tennis star **Fred Perry** not only developed his famous polo shirt, which has become a mainstay of subcultural style, but he was also one of the first men to wear shorts on the court, notably when he won the Wimbledon Championship in 1934. By the end of the decade most men had taken his lead and were playing in shorts, although Yvon Petra was the last player to wear trousers at a final as late as 1946. Until Andy Murray triumphed in 2013, Perry was the last British player to win the men's Wimbledon Championship (in 1936), and has become a tennis legend. However, he wasn't always so well respected. The son of a cotton spinner turned Labour MP, Fred was the subject of much class-based discrimination throughout his career from the elite society circles that surrounded the game, which culminated in a move to the States where he dated movie stars such as Marlene Dietrich and Jean Harlow. His eponymous polo shirt was launched in 1952, with the laurel leaf logo based on the old symbol for Wimbledon, and has never been out of style since.

An early proponent of the one-piece swimsuit was professional swimmer, film star, and vaudevillian **Annette Kellerman**. Born in Sydney, Kellerman initially took up swimming to overcome childhood paralysis. By 1902 at just 15 she was winning titles and began performing a mermaid act at the Melbourne Exhibition Aquarium. She was soon touring the world, amazing crowds with stunts such as swimming the Thames and attempting to swim the English Channel. She also performed the first water ballet in a glass tank at the New York Hippodrome, for which she is regularly credited as the inventor of synchronized swimming. Kellerman was an early proponent of practicality over modesty in swimwear, despite the social codes of the day. This culminated in her arrest in 1907 on a charge of indecent exposure on a beach in Massachusetts as her one-piece, thigh-high swimsuit was deemed far too revealing and saucy for public view. Kellerman's argument that she needed to be free from layered Victorian swimwear in order to achieve unrestricted movement was accepted by the judge and the case was dismissed. The following popularity of her one-piece swimsuit led to her own line of swimwear. No stranger to controversy, shortly after her court case Kellerman was also snapped up by Hollywood and in 1916 became the first star to appear in a nude scene. She made her mark as the professional mermaid of the film world.

The Duke of Windsor and former Prince of Wales—AKA King Edward VIII—was something of a sartorial heavyweight in the 1930s. He helped to popularize a number of checked designs including argyle through his interest in golf and golfing attire. His choices set men's trends around the globe.

Rene Lacoste was a French tennis star who dominated the game in the 1920s and 1930s along with three other players known collectively as the Four Musketeers. Nicknamed le crocodile because of the way he moved around the court, in 1933 he founded La Société Chemise Lacoste which produced his tennis shirt bearing the famous crocodile logo. Early in his career he studied the techniques of Suzanne Lenglen, and along with her he embodied 1920s chic on the court. He developed the polo shirt, the buttons and collar being an important feature as it could still look smart under his trademark deep sporty V neck jumpers. In 1933 André Merlin was the first player to wear a Lacoste polo shirt in a match, and it was soon taken up by all players.

Best known for drinking and womanizing off the pitch, footballing legend **George Best** was also known for his sartorial finesse. One of the first celebrity footballers, Best opened a series of boutiques in Manchester in the late 1960s in partnership with Manchester City's Mike Summerbee.

Chuck Taylor All-Star Converse sneakers have become such a perennial of street and fashion wear that it's often forgotten that there was a man behind the name that has lent itself to the most successful-selling basketball shoe in history. Converse began as a rubber company in the early 20th century and soon moved from winter boots to sports shoes. Charles Taylor, meanwhile, played his first professional basketball game in 1919 while he was at high school. After leaving school he became a salesman and spokesman for Converse, modifying their design in the 1920s and eventually adding his signature to the shoe in 1932. His association with Converse saw him running basketball clinics all over the USA, selling shoes at the same time as training potential stars of the game.

Esther Williams is best known as an MGM movie star of many Busby Berkeley-choreographed underwater routines. But before Hollywood called she was a competitive swimmer and set many records as a member of the Los Angeles Athletic Club swim team. Unable to compete in the 1940 Olympics due to the Second World War, she joined the spectacular Billy Rose's Aquacade where she was scouted by MGM and went on to play former swimming and celluloid star Annette Kellerman in *Million Dollar Mermaid*. After she retired from films Esther set up her own swimwear line. Still going strong today, it captures the golden age of the Hollywood musical in its retro designs.

Rock 'n' roll racing driver **James Hunt** was as well known in the 1970s for his scruffy-yet-stylish look (that often included bare feet and worn denim) as he was for winning the Formula One World Championship in 1976. Another sporting playboy, his sartorial edge is still referenced in fashion shows today, such as a recent Trussardi collection that referenced iconic drivers of the 1970s including Hunt's contemporary Jackie Stewart.

The idea of sports personality product tie-ins was taken to a whole new level in the 1980s with **Michael Jordan** and Nike. Michael Jordan, an up-and-coming basketball star, had previously worn Converse sneakers and was initially keen to work with Adidas on promoting their footwear. However, Nike were actively looking for new marketing strategies as the running boom of the 1970s was petering out, so they were eager to enter the endorsement arena. From a series of meetings an arrangement was made, and the now-famous Air Jordan was born—complete with design tweaks from Jordan himself. Nike spent an unprecedented amount on the campaign, including direct advertising featuring Jordan as well as paying him to wear the product. In the 1984–85 season the NBA ruled against wearing the red-and-black design on the court as they flouted color regulations, and Jordan was charged $5000 for every game that he wore them. Nike happily footed the bill for such publicity. Jordan played a great season and won Rookie of the Year; by the time Air Jordans went on sale in 1985 they couldn't be stocked fast enough and they remain one of the top-selling basketball trainers in the world today. It was a defining moment in the history of celebrity endorsement and the marketing of sportswear.

The pin-up of the "metrosexual" moniker, **David Beckham** was as famous for his hairstyles, licensing deals, and at times controversial fashion choices as he was for his moves on the pitch. It was headline news when he wore a sarong in 1998, and again the following year when he adopted a Versace leather outfit that matched with his wife—and fellow fashion heavyweight—Victoria.

Self-styled bad boy of basketball Dennis Rodman is well known for his eccentric appearance, which has included dying his hair a different color for every game and wearing a wedding dress to promote his autobiography in the mid 1990s.

The Williams sisters are certainly no shrinking violets when it comes to style on the tennis court. **Venus**, having sported such unlikely ensembles as a lace playsuit, a blood-red frilled dress, and a sheer number embellished with diamanté spider's webs, is the designer behind her own line, EleVen. Far from a novice, she has a degree in fashion and has collaborated in the past with design powerhouses such as Diane von Furstenberg and Ralph Lauren. Keen to bring print and pattern to traditional tennis whites, her motto is "if you don't look good, you won't play well" and she has shown her range at New York fashion week. Younger sister **Serena** is also no stranger to the style spotlight; she has designed her own line ANERES, is a qualified nail technician, and is also known for her flamboyant outfit choices on the court.

Cuthbert Collingwood Tinling, best known as **Ted Tinling**, began his tennis career in the south of France as personal umpire to Suzanne Lenglen. He went on to design iconic dresses for the game, throughout his career he designed for almost all the top female players from the 1950s to the 1970s, including Martina Navratilova and Billie Jean King. His eye-catching designs weren't always looked upon favorably by the Wimbledon establishment, but nevertheless he gained industry acceptance and went on to become a consultant and liaison to the players. After his death it was also discovered that he had been a spy for British Intelligence during the Second World War.

Throughout the 1920s **Bobby Jones** was an American amateur golfer whose standards of fair play combined with his sporting excellence have seen him go down in history as an archetype of great sportsmanship and sartorial flair. He competed successfully against the world's top professional golfers and he dominated competitions to become the most successful amateur golfer ever: by profession he was a lawyer and he never gave up the day job.

The little known **Gloria Minoprio** was a golfer-turned-magician in the 1930s who scandalized society by being the first female golfer to play in trousers, flouting the rules of the Ladies' Golf Union. Her methods of play were also unconventional; she used a single golf club to play across all terrain. In later years she travelled to India and performed her magic acts for the Maharajas.

> "Clothes make the man. Naked people have little or no influence on society." MARK TWAIN

Skateboarder and surfer **Stacy Peralta** first turned pro in the early 1970s, and helped to set the laid-back look that has since come to define skate style. Toward the end of the decade he teamed up with George Powell to create the Powell-Peralta skate gear company, which still operates today selling clothing and other skate goods. He also formed the Bones Brigade, a team of the best skaters of the time. An accomplished director, he has several films under his belt, including acclaimed documentaries on skating (*Dogtown and Z-Boys*, 2001), surfing (*Riding Giants*, 2004), and gang culture (*Crips and Bloods: Made in America*, 2008). With his casual style and merchandize tie-ins, Peralta paved the way for future pro-skaters to launch clothing and product lines, such as Tony Hawk, a fellow Bones Brigade member.

A BRIEF GUIDE TO... COLORS

S HOCKING PINK was invented by Elsa Schiaparelli in 1937 to grace the box of her latest perfume, "Shocking." It was inspired by the Tête de Belier (Ram's Head): a 17.27ct pink diamond from Cartier, owned by one of Schiaparelli's favorite clients, heiress Daisy Fellowes.

Jeanne Lanvin was mesmerized by the frescos of Fra Angelico on a trip to Florence, especially the use of "quattrocento blue." Adapting it into her designs, the cornflower shade would thereafter be known as Lanvin blue.

Black was the color of mourning until Coco Chanel put it on the fashion map in 1926.

Mauveine was the name of the first synthetic organic chemical dye. Discovered in 1856 by William Henry Perkin as he was attempting to synthesize an anti-malaria drug. Perkin patented the method and opened a dyeworks. The color was given a huge boost in 1862 when Queen Victoria wore a mauve-dyed dress to a Royal Exhibition. Within 50 years of the discovery 2000 artificial aniline dyes were in existence, which revolutionized the palette of fashion.

Tyrian purple, also known as royal or imperial purple, has been associated with the nobility since antiquity. The secretion of a species of sea snail, the reddish-purple color was prized for remaining bright despite exposure to sun and weather. Extracting the substance, or crushing the snails, was a very labor-intensive process, leading to high prices and social status. For this reason purple has been the subject of many sumptuary laws and restrictions throughout its history.

Magenta was another early aniline dye originally called fuchsine in 1858. The name was changed after the Battle of Magenta on 4th June 1859, a key victory for the French-Sardinian troops during the Second Italian War of Independence.

Indigo: the genus of plants known as indigofera has been harvested in India since 3000 BC for its deep, rich, long-lasting blue color, making it the oldest dyestuff known to humanity. In the mid 16th century it was introduced to Europe where it replaced woad as the plant-of-choice to create blue dye. For centuries its ease of manufacture and low cost made it the staple color of workwear, yet its back-story has a much darker tone. The crop flourished in the climate of the southern United States and Caribbean, and from the mid 18th century it became one of the first colonial exports to turn a profit, when harvested by slave labor. Gandhi also took up the plight of oppressed Indigo workers early in his campaign for Indian independence. This became central to his message in later years, advocating that people wear only undyed homespun cotton.

PRINT TERMINOLOGY 3

PAPER IMPRESSION: Before cloth is printed a test run is performed using paper so the factory can keep a record of it and check for any irregularities that would be costly to amend on fabric. These impressions often survive in the pattern books of printing mills.

PATIO PRINTS: Large-scale floral patterns originally produced in the 1940s and 1950s. Typically found on heavy-weight cotton known as bark cloth, they feature bright, bold prints that were often tropical or exotic, as such they tapped into the leisure boom of the postwar years.

SWATCH/PATTERN BOOK: Textile mills tradi-tionally keep annual or seasonal records of their production that contain samples of their designs. Often this takes the form of paper impressions, but it may also include fabric swatches or gouache designs.

TOILE DE JOUY: The first copperplate printed toiles were made in Ireland in 1752. But Toile de Jouy referred to the mill owned by Christophe-Philippe Oberkampf in Jouy, near Versailles, from where the best examples were said to originate; they were produced from 1783 and specialized in pastoral scenes among others. Oberkampf hired the best artists of the time to design his prints, and they even decorated the house in Washington DC owned by the president of the recently-independent America.

TROMPE L'OEIL: Literally "deceive the eye," this is a design technique that is used throughout the decorative arts to create the illusion that flat surfaces are three-dimensional. In textile printing, this can take the form of "3D objects" on or interacting with the fabric, or it can be used to make fabrics resemble other fabrics, such as check and plaids, embroidery or watered silk.

TURKEY-REDS: Also known as Adrianople reds, initially the term referred to the color of dye, but soon came to mean the whole print. Taken from the root of the rubia plant, the color created was more vibrant than the earlier madder red, but the process was complicated and timely. Originating in either India or Turkey, it became associated with the bright colors of the Ottoman Empire and the name stuck. In 1810 a discharge print technique was developed to create black and blue patterns onto the fiery background, and yellow was later added. The patterns are usually bright, starburst florals or paisleys, and European examples were particularly popular for export to the Russian market.

VERMICULAR: A coral-like design that has been likened to the tracks of worms since Roman times. Origin: Latin *vermiculari* means to be full of worms.

PHONETIC FASHION

NEVER BE CAUGHT OUT AGAIN with this handy guide to pronouncing your favorite designers:

ANYA HINDMARCH:
Ahn-ya Hinde-march

PROENZA SCHOULER:
Pro-enza Skoola

PRABAL GURUNG: Prubble
(as in "trouble") Gerr-oong

BALENCIAGA: Bal-en-si-ahga

RODARTE: Ro-dar-tay

ANDREW GN: Andrew Jen

HUSSEIN CHALAYAN:
Huuss-ain (as in "rain")
Sha-lye-uhn

THAKOON: Ta-koon

CHLOË SEVIGNY FOR O.C.:
Klow-ee Seven-ee for O.C.
(Opening Ceremony)

MEADHAM KIRCHHOFF:
Meed-am Kirtch-off

DRIES VAN NOTEN:
Dreeze van Noht-en

GIVENCHY: Jzhe-von-shee

HERMES: air-mezz

LANVIN: Lon-van

LOEWE: Low-eh-veh

MARCHESA: Mar-kay-zah

MOSCHINO: Moss-keen-oh

OLIVIER THEYSKENS:
Oliv-iyay Teskins

THIERRY MUGLER:
Tee-airy Moog-lair

ROKSANDA ILINCIC:
Rok-sanda Ee-lin-chich

ROLAND MOURET:
Roland Mour-ay

SONIA RYKIEL: Son-ya
Ree-ki-el

SASS & BIDE: Sass and Bide
(as in "bide your time")

VERONIQUE BRANQUINHO:
Ver-on-eek Bran-keen-o

VERSACE: Ver-sar-chay

"The best thing about London, is Paris." DIANA VREELAND

FASHION GEOGRAPHY FROM OFF-THE-BEATEN TRACK

THROUGHOUT THE 20TH CENTURY the fashion industry remained focused on Paris, London, New York, and later Milan. But with the rise of the internet and the frequency of international travel, fashion is no longer as reliant on the four traditional style centers. Here are some picks from the global world of fashion design.

BELGIUM: Though not situated far from Europe's fashion centers, Antwerp's Royal Academy of Fine Arts produced a crop of designers with a distinct aesthetic in the early 1980s, who collectively became known as the "Antwerp Six:" Walter Van Beirendonck, Ann Demeulemeester, Dries Van Noten, Dirk Van Saene, Dirk Bikkembergs, and Marina Yee. In the face of the disco and Studio 54-inspired designs of the late 1970s and the label mania of the 1980s, they opted for a pared down, androgynous, deconstruction-based approach. Though not a member of the Six, Martin Margiela is also associated with the creative outpouring of Antwerp; his vision offers a radical reinterpretation of fashion that has since become associated with Belgian design.

JAPAN: The domination of Europe and the States was also called into question in the 1980s by what has been dubbed the Japanese "fashion revolution." Bringing an avant-garde aesthetic that featured minimalism, a predilection for black and the influence of traditional techniques fused with cutting-edge technology, designers such as Yohji Yamamoto, Issey Miyake, and Rei Kawakubo of Commes des Garçons forged a brave new world on the catwalks of Paris. For Miyake's seminal "Please Please" collections he was inspired by traditional Japanese traveling coats that were made of paper. Rei Kawakubo's cerebral approach was epitomized in the "Body Meets Dress, Dress Meets Body" collection from 1997. Paying homage to Western fashions of the 18th and 19th century, Kawakubo created her own take on the extreme femininity of the age by misappropriating bustles and padding to extreme effect.

NIGERIA: Designer Lisa Folawigo began the Jewel by Lisa label in 2005. Inspired by the Ankara prints that are traditionally associated with west Africa, Folawigo has created her own custom designs and turned the print into a high-fashion fabric. Showing her collections all over the world as well as at Lagos Fashion Week, she also uses traditional techniques such as hand embellishment and beading.

TURKEY: The Eternal Child knitwear label was founded by Istanbul-based designer Gül Gürdamar who studied at Central Saint Martins. She is influenced by the Galata District, an older region of the city that has retained its 19th-century feel.

DENMARK: Scandinavia has a rich history of pared back luxury, and Danish label Noir is no exception. Referencing mystique and power as well as the color black, the Noir aesthetic focuses on clean lines and nurtures a sophisticated, contemporary brand of femininity.

BOTSWANA: Accessories label TswanaLyric was set up in 2007 in Gaborone. Fusing African heritage with a contemporary feel, the statement jewelry brand was a finalist for the British Council/London Fashion Week Emerging Talent Award 2012.

ARGENTINA: Buenos Aires-born Pablo Ramirez launched his label in 2000. With a growing reputation on the world stage, he is the recipient of numerous awards resulting in staging his collections all over the globe.

CHINA: Selling in stores from Moscow to London, Shanghai-based designer Uma Wang was labeled "China's hottest emerging designer" by influential website Business of Fashion and is known for her oversize, layered knitwear. Designer Yang Du is based in London but grew up in Dalian, North China. Known for her playful, kitsch designs she has a cartoon-like aesthetic that has won her fans among London's street style-loving cognoscenti. Showing at Beijing Fashion Week, designer Liang Zi has won awards for her use of "gambiered" Canton silk—a 500-year-old hand dye technique.

KOREA: Born and brought up in South Korea, Yeashin Kim launched the Yeashin brand in 2012 after graduating from London College of Fashion. Mixing 1960s mod style with traditional Korean costume, the result is a vibrant mix of color and texture.

BRAZIL: Lucas Nascimento hails from Bonito in Brazil and showed at Rio Fashion Week before transferring to London (where he also studied) to be awarded NEWGEN sponsorship (funded by Topshop) to show his collection at London Fashion Week. Creating structured pieces with a futuristic feel, he brings an original take to knitwear design.

AUSTRALIA: In 2005 designers Luke Sales and Anna Plunkett launched their label Romance Was Born with a focus on intricate and bold statement prints and hand-finishing. Stocked in boutiques from Hong Kong and Tokyo to New York, they regularly show at Australian Fashion Week in Sydney where they recently premiered a collection supported by MARVEL comics. Designer Alice Edgeley established her label Edgeley after working in London for Christopher Kane and designing costume for theater and live performance. Returning to Melbourne she set up her boutique where the label continues to thrive, referencing forgotten moments of fashion history through a contemporary perspective.

RUSSIA: Growing up in St Petersburg, Timur Kim showed his first fashion collection at the age of just 16. Following studies at Central Saint Martins, he has created capsule collections in collaboration with Pringle of Scotland and cites his inspirations as ranging from early 20th-century Russia to cowboys.

INDIA: Based between Paris and New Delhi, Manish Arora first launched his label in 1997 and showed at the first ever India Fashion Week in 2000. Often dubbed the "John Galliano of India," Arora's aesthetic fuses Western silhouettes with the bright colors of the Indian subcontinent as well as traditional crafts such as appliqué, beading, and embroidery. He was briefly the creative director at the relaunched design house Paco Rabanne.

HOW TO... TIE A BOW TIE

1 Take the end in your left hand and extend the tie 2.5–3 cm below the end in your right hand.

2 Cross the longer end over the shorter end and bring it up through the loop.

3 Create a front loop by doubling up the shorter end and laying it across the collar points.

4 Hold the front loop with the left thumb and forefinger and let the long end drop over the front.

5 Put the right forefinger on the bottom half of the hanging end, pointing up. Pass it up from the front loop.

6 Poke the resulting loop through the knot that lies behind the front loop. Make sure the ends are even and tighten to fit.

"Fashion is not necessarily about labels. It's not about brands. It's about something else that comes from within you." RALPH LAUREN

BEHIND THE SEAMS: FASHION DOCUMENTARIES 3

GREY GARDENS (Dir. Maysles Brothers, 1975): An eccentric film about the aunt and cousin of Jackie O living in a decaying mansion in East Hampton. Little Edie's habit of using sweaters as hats, and skirts as capes has been cited as an inspiration for countless designers and stylists.

SEAMLESS (Dir. Douglas Keeve, 2005): From the director of *Unzipped*, this is a look at young fashion designers in New York and what it takes to make it in the industry.

VIDAL SASSOON: THE MOVIE (Dir. Craig Teper, 2010): An insider look at the man who revolutionized hairdressing and maintenance in the 1960s and helped to put "Swinging London" on the map alongside Mary Quant.

YVES SAINT LAURENT: HIS LIFE AND TIMES, AND YVES SAINT LAURENT 5 AVENUE MARCEAU 75116 PARIS (Dir. David Teboul, 2002): This double bill about French designer Yves Saint Laurent showcases his life and career, and 60 days inside his couture house respectively. A third documentary, *L'Amour Fou*, (Dir. Pierre Thoretton, 2009) was made after his death, featuring interviews with his business partner and lover, Pierre Berge.

BILL CUNNINGHAM NEW YORK (Dir. Richard Press, 2010): Cunningham has become an iconic sight on the streets of the Big Apple as he shoots for his New York Times column. This is a candid portrait of the industry's first streetstyle photographer, now a legendary industry figure.

IN VOGUE: THE EDITOR'S EYE (Dir. Fenton Bailey and Randy Barbato, 2012): Hot on the heels of the success of *The September Issue*, *The Editor's Eye* focuses on the stories behind iconic images from *Vogue*, as recounted by it's endlessly entertaining editors.

SCATTER MY ASHES AT BERGDORF'S (Dir. Matthew Miele, 2013): A peak at the inner workings of one of the fashion industry's best-loved department stores, featuring everyone from Tom Ford and Giorgio Armani to Joan Rivers and the Olsen Twins.

ABOUT FACE: SUPERMODELS THEN AND NOW (Dir. Timothy Greenfield-Sanders, 2012): In an industry criticized for its shallow reliance on looks, this is an exploration of aging through the stories of women who have defined our ideas of beauty for decades.

CUT OF YOUR JIB

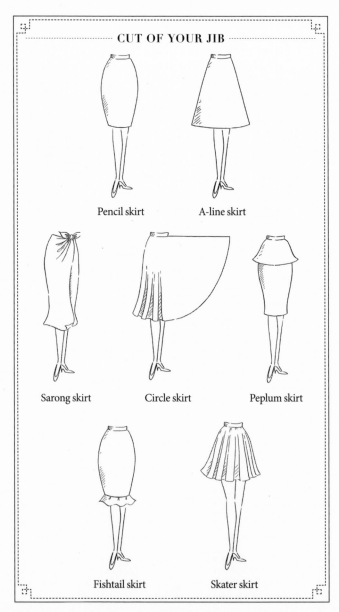

Pencil skirt

A-line skirt

Sarong skirt

Circle skirt

Peplum skirt

Fishtail skirt

Skater skirt

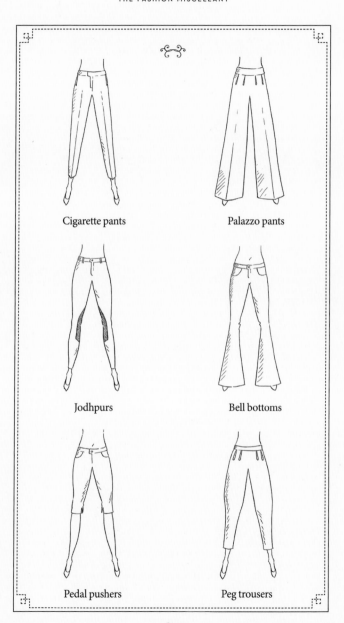

Cigarette pants

Palazzo pants

Jodhpurs

Bell bottoms

Pedal pushers

Peg trousers

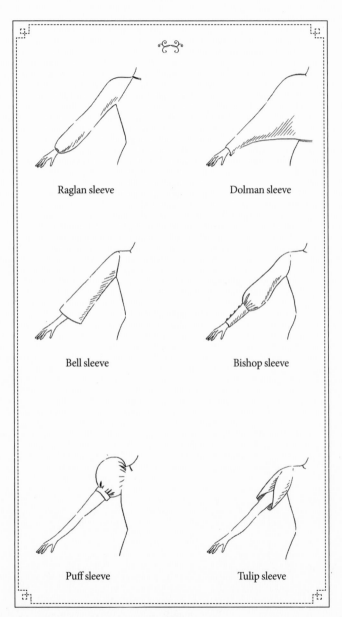

Raglan sleeve

Dolman sleeve

Bell sleeve

Bishop sleeve

Puff sleeve

Tulip sleeve

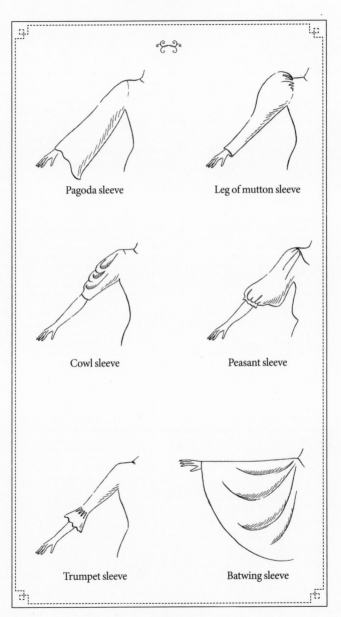

Pagoda sleeve

Leg of mutton sleeve

Cowl sleeve

Peasant sleeve

Trumpet sleeve

Batwing sleeve

FASHION ON FILM 3

CLEOPATRA (DIR. JOSEPH L. MANKIEWICZ, 1963): Going down in movie history as one of the most expensive films ever made, the film is notorious for nearly bankrupting 20th Century Fox. Liz Taylor defined the 1960s with her kohl-heavy eye makeup. From her 65 elaborate costumes, one was even made of 24-carat gold cloth.

CLUELESS (DIR. AMY HECKERLING, 1995): The ultimate makeover movie. Based on Jane Austen's *Emma*, *Clueless* is forever immortalized for popularizing matchy-matchy yellow plaid and highlighting the importance of Calvin Klein and Azzedine Alaïa to the otherwise slacker Generation X.

BLOW-UP (DIR. MICHELANGELO ANTONIONI, 1966): Part inspired by bad boy photographer David Bailey, *Blow-Up* sees David Hemmings playing a photographer embroiled in a murder. Featuring a cameo from The Yardbirds and a starring role from model Veruschka, the film is a snapshot of London's glamorous swinging 1960s fashion scene.

METROPOLIS (DIR. FRITZ LANG, 1927): The angular cityscapes of this German Expressionist masterpiece continue to influence designers from Riccardo Tisci at Givenchy to Donatella Versace and Holly Fulton.

BREATHLESS (DIR, JEAN LUC GODARD, 1960): French cinema's *Nouvelle Vague* was given a kick start with Jean Luc Godard's first feature-length film. With Jean Seberg in the starring role, it helped to make pixie cuts and Breton stripes a defining look of the 1960s.

MARNIE (DIR. ALFRED HITCHCOCK, 1964): Hitchcock's icy blondes—especially Tippi Hedren—when clad in tightly cinched Edith Head suits are a perennial source of inspiration for designers like John Galliano and Alice Temperley.

BARBARELLA (DIR. ROGER VADIM, 1968): As if the presence of 1960s style icon Anita Pallenberg wasn't enough, Paco Rabanne's help with the costumes for this intergalactic kitschfest ensures it has a secure place in the fashion hall of fame.

JUBILEE (DIR. DEREK JARMAN, 1978): Jarman's cult film fuses Shakespeare and Elizabeth I with a nihilistic look at late 1970s punk-infused London, featuring performers Adam Ant and Toyah Willcox and with cameo appearances by The Slits and Siouxsie and the Banshees. The film was also scored by Brian Eno.

AMERICAN GIGOLO (DIR. PAUL SCHRADER, 1980): Richard Gere popularized Armani's deconstructed suits that perfectly showed off his gym-honed body in this film whose materialistic decadence would come to characterize the yuppie lifestyle of the 1980s.

A SINGLE MAN (DIR. TOM FORD, 2009): Designer Tom Ford took his appreciation of color and tone to the big screen with his award-winning directorial debut. Set in the early 1960s, it tapped into the zeitgeist by using the same production design team as *Mad Men*.

ZOOLANDER (DIR. BEN STILLER, 2001): Arguably the best fashion spoof, Derek Zoolander brought us the famous "Blue Steel" look and parodied the industry's predilection for beauty over brains.

QUADROPHENIA (DIR. FRANC RODDAM, 1979): Loosely based on an earlier rock opera by The Who, *Quadrophenia* chronicled the clash between Mods and Rockers at Brighton beach and sparked a Mod revival that was still being felt in the heyday of 1990s Britpop.

LIBERTY AESTHETICS

FOUNDED IN 1875, Liberty quickly established itself as one of the most fashionable stores in London. By the 1880s Arthur Lasenby Liberty was importing plain silks from the Middle and Far East and dying them in Britain, creating a range of muted "Liberty colors" that were associated with the Aesthetic Dress movement. Aesthetic Dress—an evolution of the Artistic Dress of the Pre-Raphaelites earlier in the century—was characterized by a partial rejection of the corset in favor of unstructured lines, and the use of natural colors rather than the garish aniline dyes that were in vogue at the time. This encouraged a return to anti-industrialist vegetable dyes, which produced a color palette of antique-looking shades. The association of Liberty with Aesthetic Dress was so strong that when Gilbert and Sullivan's comic opera "Patience" premiered in 1881—satirizing the Aesthetic movement—the costumes were made from Liberty fabrics, and they were even advertised in the program. Well known for its signature fabrics, Nouveau, paisley and floral prints, and its striking use of color, Liberty remains one of the top shopping destinations in London.

> *"Elegance is the only beauty that never fades."*
> AUDREY HEPBURN

-------------------------------- PRINT TECHNIQUES --------------------------------

3D PRINTING: Or 3D modeling, this technique takes input digitally from 3D data and creates 3D replicas through a virtual blueprint and layer-by-layer process. It's now possible to 3D print a vast array of accessories and even fabric.

BLOCK PRINTING: By the late Middle Ages block-printing was an established trade in Europe, although its origins date back to antiquity. The print design is carved in relief onto wooden blocks; a different block is used for each color. Cloth is stretched taut on a padded table and the block face is pressed against a dye-saturated sieve then applied to the fabric. A strike from a mallet to the back of the block transfers the design onto the fabric. The block is then moved along and the method is repeated. Very rarely used today as the process is so labor-intensive.

COPPERPLATE PRINTING: Developed in the mid-18th century in Britain and Ireland, this process allows for more detail than block printing. The design is engraved onto a flat copper plate that is then rubbed with printing dye. The dye is wiped from the surface, so it only remains in the indented lines of the engraving. Cloth is laid over the plate and pressure is applied by a mechanical press to transfer the design to the fabric. Due to this innovation, larger-scale prints could be created (with block printing there was a limit depending on the weight of block the printer could carry), and it also enabled finer-scale prints, which led to the development of scenic toiles.

DIGITAL PRINTING: Direct-to-garment digital printing is a variant of inkjet printing when applied to textiles from an image generated on computer. As the process is controlled by computer rather than the hand it allows for more complex patterns and is more precise.

MORDANT-DYE TECHNIQUES: A mordant is an agent that makes a dye permanent or colorfast. Techniques for this were unknown in Europe until the early 18th century, and the domestic market for colorfast fabrics drove much of the textile trade with India, who had developed methods much earlier.

PERROTINE PRINTING: The perrotine press was invented in Rouen (France) in 1834 as a process for mechanizing block printing. The process prints several colors at once, transferring the color to the blocks, stamping the fabric and moving it forward for the next impression. Although it's faster and more accurate than traditional block printing, it retains a handcrafted look as the blocks are still carved by hand.

PICOTAGE, OR PINNING: For finer detailing on woodblock prints, brass pins were stuck into the blocks to create areas of intricate dotting that could be used as an effect on its own or to create light and dark shading.

RESIST DYEING: A paste or wax that is resistant to dye is printed or painted onto cloth. The cloth is then fully dyed and the resist is removed. Where the resist has stopped the dye from penetrating, the cloth will be left its original color, creating an inverse effect to regular print techniques. Batik is a popular version of this method using wax. Tie-dye is another version (see below).

ROLLER PRINTING: This was the starting point for the mass production of printing methods. In 1783, Thomas Bell patented the first machine to use engraved metal rollers, which essentially mechanized fabric-printing. Most western mills were using roller printers by the 1820s, as a six-color roller printer did the work of 40 hand-block printers. A diamond-pointed pantograph was used to transfer the design to a copper cylinder coated in acid-resistant varnish; the exposed lines of the pattern were etched into the copper roller when the cylinder was revolved in an acid bath. The printing press also ran cloth under the rollers in a continuous sheet. A photographic process has been used since the late 1950s to engrave the rollers, which has eliminated the need for a skilled engraver. Today machines can print up to 18 colors at a time. The roller printer put textile printing at the cutting edge of the industrial revolution by making it the first fully mechanized industry.

SCREEN PRINTING: Commercial manual silk-screen printing began in the 1920s. The technique is useful for short runs of high fashion fabrics as it's faster than block printing yet more affordable than roller printing in small runs. A fine mesh cloth is stretched taut onto a frame. The pattern is created by painting out the background with a protective varnish, then color is added with a squeegee that presses through the screen onto the cloth below; each color has a separate screen. Most practitioners now use a photographic process where the design is "developed" onto the screen. From the 1960s onwards this method faced competition from rotary-screen printing, which transfers the screen from silk to a cylindrical fine metal mesh.

TIE-DYE: Associated with the "Summer of Love" and nostalgic late 1960s styles, tie-dye actually has a much older lineage. The ancient hand-dyeing technique is known as "plangi" in Indonesia, "bandhana" in India, and "shibori" in Japan and involves tightly tying or winding fabric so as to leave patterns of the original color after the fabric is dipped in dye. This look can also be reproduced mechanically.

WARP PRINTING: Warp is the vertical yarn on a weaver's loom. When the warp threads are printed before the weft threads are woven in, the print is left with a fuzzy, slightly out-of-focus look. Also known as "shadow silks" as this effect is most often found on silk.

INDEX

INDEX

INDEX

ACKNOWLEDGMENTS

Rob Flowers, William Smith, Morwenna Ferrier, Emma Bowkett